Da Curse of the Billy Goat

The Chicago Cubs, Pennant Races, and Curses

Chicago Tribune File Photograph

Da Curse of the Billy Goat

The Chicago Cubs, Pennant Races, and Curses

Steve Gatto

To John White,
Go Cubs!

[signature]

Protar

House

P.O. Box 14007
Lansing, Michigan 48901

Copyright © by Steve Gatto.

ISBN #0-9720910-4-1 (Softcover)

First Edition: March 2004

**Protar House
P.O. Box 14007
Lansing, Michigan 48901**

CONTENTS

Acknowledgments   vii

1. Enter The Goat   1
2. Tinker To Evers To Chance   7
3. The Curse Years   15
4. The Big Hurt   19
5. Wait Till Next Year   29
6. The Miracle Season   37
7. The Boys Of Zimmer   53
8. Lifting The Curse   57
9. Year Of The Goat   65
10. Truth About Baseball Curses   77

Epilogue   83
Notes and Sources   87
Bibliography   103
Index   109

Acknowledgments

I would like to thank the many institutions throughout the country for their continuing work in preserving a wealth of documents that enable researchers to find details about historical characters and incidents. The newspaper collections housed in the Chicago Public Library and Library of Michigan are valuable resources to anyone researching the history of Chicago. In addition, the Chicago Historical Society provided much material for review. Also, in this modern age, Internet resources like Baseball-Reference.com, ChicagoCubs.com, ChicagoSports.com, ESPN.com, MLB.com, and a host of other sites, are valuable resources for researching information.

No research on this subject could be done without the various Chicago newspapers that have been published since 1908. Some of these newspapers no longer exist or have merged with other newspapers, but much of the material they published throughout the years has been preserved on microfilm. Among these I would like to recognize the work and dedication of the staffs of the *Chicago Daily News, Chicago Herald-American, Chicago Sun, Chicago Sun-Times, Chicago Times, Chicago Tribune, Detroit Free Press,* and *New York Times*. I would like to give special thanks to the reprint permissions departments of the *Chicago Tribune* and *Chicago Sun-Times* for their assistance in obtaining photographs and permission for their use, from their respective publications.

Ted Liliensteins deserves special thanks for his work on the cover illustration for this book.

The Chicago Cubs deserve recognition for the many years of joy and elation they have provided to their fans, who share in the club's quest to again win a National League pennant and World Series Championship.

Sam Sianis, owner of the famous Billy Goat Tavern in Chicago, deserves acknowledgment for the key role he has played throughout the years relating to the Curse of the Billy Goat. Moreover, his preservation of the Billy Goat Tavern, a Chicago landmark, with the newspaper articles and other ephemera on the walls, allows visitors to the city to get a feel for the history of Chicago.

Finally, a special thanks goes out to William "Billy Goat" Sianis, who after being ejected from the 1945 World Series, started the Curse of the Billy Goat. The hex he uttered has grown from a Chicago urban legend to one of the most famous curses in baseball history. Today, Billy Goat Sianis and the Curse of the Billy Goat are inextricably intertwined with the history of Chicago and the lore of the Chicago Cubs.

1

ENTER THE GOAT

On Friday, October 5, 1945, the Chicago Cubs, after playing the first three games of the 1945 World Series in Detroit, returned by train to Chicago for the fourth game in the series with a one-game lead over the Tigers. A huge crowd at Union Station eagerly awaited the arrival of the National League Champions.[1] Excitement was high because it had been seven years since Wrigley Field had hosted a World Series game and thirty-seven years since the Cubs had won the 1908 World Series.[2]

In preparation for the gala event, Wrigley Field underwent an impressive makeover to attain a look of perfection—"from the bunting-swathed rails of the lower boxes and upper grandstand to the pennant festooned cables that do a two-way stretch from the top of the center field scoreboard to the bleacher corners."[3] The grass was trimmed and the infield was neatly manicured before two waterproof tarpaulins were laid out to protect the baselines, home plate, and the infield area.

Chicago fans were anxious to see their beloved Cubs finally win another World Series, and there was a rush in the city for tickets to the ballgame. Additional chairs were added to the box seat section, increasing the seating capacity to 41,700. Another 2,500 standing-room-only admission tickets were also to be offered. Scalpers were out on the streets, inflating ticket prices. "Choice box seats at Wrigley Field are said to be bringing scalpers as much as $200 a set, and long-apportioned reserved grandstand seats are attracting upwards of $75," noted one sportswriter.[4] Baseball die-hards stood in line all night in thirty-degree weather waiting for bleacher seats to go on sale in the morning.[5]

One fan with two $7.20 box seat tickets was William Sianis, nicknamed "Billy Goat" for the goatee he wore.[6] Sianis was a Greek immigrant who owned the nearby Lincoln Tavern on West Madison Street. Over the next twenty-five years he would earn a reputation in Chicago as a shrewd businessman, and his renamed Billy Goat Tavern would become a Chicago landmark.[7] According to one story, Billy Goat Sianis purchased his tavern in 1934 "with a $200 check from someone who owed him and $5 of his own money."[8] The check bounced, but Sianis later paid it off with sales from his first week in business. When the Republican Convention was held in Chicago one year, he reportedly put up a sign at his tavern stating that he did not serve Republicans. The next day at lunch, the tavern, as one might expect, was filled with eager Republican customers who forced their money on him.[9] Sianis at one point even wrote a letter to the State Department requesting the first "food-and-drink license" for the moon.[10]

But Sianis is most famous for the day he came to Wrigley Field with two box seat tickets for the fourth game of the 1945 World Series. One ticket was for himself and the other for his pet goat Murphy, which Sianis had reportedly taken in after the animal jumped off a truck near his tavern.[11] He apparently brought the goat to Wrigley Field to give the Cubs luck; however, it is likely that Sianis, a master of promotion, also conjured up the stunt to promote his tavern.

Some accounts claim that William Sianis' pet goat was denied entry into Wrigley Field that day. In actuality, the combined effort of a squad of ushers at the stadium failed to keep "Sianis and his pet billy goat out of the ball park."[12] The goat's appearance on the playing field before the game caught the attention of rain-soaked fans who anxiously awaited the start of the game with hopes that it would not be cancelled due to the wet weather. Wrigley Field ushers, who were using walkie-talkies to communicate with each other for crowd control, intervened to end the stunt, converging on Sianis and his pet goat.[13] The ushers then led the pair to the grandstand aisle, but the animal ran back onto the field.[14] Recognizing the uproar the goat was causing, photographers began snapping pictures of the animal as it posed on the field and roamed near the visiting dugout before finally being escorted off the playing field. The ushers attempted to remove the animal from the stadium, but Sianis argued that he had paid for two box seats and maintained that there was no disclaimer on the tickets preventing him from using one for his goat. After a heated argument, Sianis and the animal were allowed to occupy the box seats for which he had tickets.[15]

Rain initially delayed the game for about ten minutes, but by the fifth inning the sun began to shine through the clouds. Thirty-nine-year-old southpaw Ray Prim managed to get out the first ten Detroit batters in order before the Tigers began hitting the ball. Detroit's Paul "Dizzy" Trout used "a fast-breaking sinker which he mixed with a fastball so effectively that the Cubs could connect for only five hits."[16] The Tigers beat the Cubs and evened the series at two games apiece.

The following day, October 7, 1945, the *Chicago Times* and the *Chicago Tribune* ran stories that mentioned the billy goat incident at Wrigley Field. An article by Gene Kessler, sports editor for the *Times*, featured a photograph of Sianis waving his hat at the crowd while in his box seat with his goat. The caption read: "This goat had a seat—This goat causes uproar in Wrigley field yesterday, but is permitted to stay put in box seat after owner, 'Billy Goat' Sianis, tavern owner, protests animal's being given bum's rush by ushers." Kessler's additional comments about the goat incident provided more detail regarding what occurred at Wrigley Field:

> A goat wearing the sign: "We got Detroit's goat," was brought on the field. All the goat got was good and wet, but seemed to enjoy it until two Andy Frain ushers [employees of Andy Frain's security company] took him into custody. The ushers led Billy to the head of the grandstand aisle, but Mr. Goat balked, turned around and insisted on going back to the field. He got his wish when photographers asked that he return for poses and the goat wound up proudly roaming close to the visiting dugout while cameras snapped.

Finally, the goat was permitted to stay in his owner's box after a heated argument. The owner, Billy Sianis, who operates a tavern, argued that he had purchased a box seat for his goat and there was nothing printed on the ticket which said he couldn't use it for an animal.

While flourishing the ticket, Mr. Goat grabbed for it and Andy Frain remarked: "If he eats the ticket that would solve everything."

He didn't eat the pasteboard and stayed in the seat.

Although the *Times* article did not mention it, Sianis and his goat were ejected from the stadium prior to the end of the game, reportedly because of the animal's objectionable odor. About the goat's ejection, Arch Ward of the *Tribune* stated:

> Andy Frain [head of the security company] employed 525 ushers and other attendants to handle the capacity throng.... He had trouble with only one fan, Billy Sianis, owner of a tavern near Chicago Stadium, who insisted on bringing a goat into the box seat section.... Sianis had a ticket for the goat, which was paraded thru the American league area of front box customers.... The critter wore a blanket on which was pinned a sign reading 'We Got Detroit's Goat.'... Frain finally convinced Sianis goats should be with the Navy football teams.[17]

Sianis was outraged by the ejection, and in response, he placed a curse upon the Cubs. Some accounts claim that Sianis pronounced that the World Series would never be played in Wrigley Field again. Other accounts allege that "an indignant Sianis stood outside the stadium and cursed the team, vowing it would never again return to the World Series."[18] Sianis' family maintains that he "sent a telegram to Mr.

Wrigley saying, 'You are going to lose this World Series and you are never going to go to another World Series again. You are never going to win a World Series again because you insulted my goat.'"[19]

On Tuesday, October 9, 1945, *Chicago Times* columnist Irv Kupcinet described the goat incident in his "Kup's Column:"

> William (Billy Goat) Sianis the W. Madison st. tavern owner, created a stir at Wrigley field Sunday when he led his pet goat into the ball park and then insisted on having the animal occupy the seat next to him. He pleaded to no avail that he spent $7.20 for a box seat for his pet goat.... Ushers finally evicted the goat, over Sianis' strong protests. After Detroit defeated the Cubs, 8-4, Sianis sent P. K. Wrigley this wire: "Who smells now?"

The Cubs eventually lost the 1945 World Series when they were soundly beaten in game seven. Publicly there was little talk, if any, of the so-called Curse of the Billy Goat being the cause of the Cubbies' demise. Nonetheless, with the passage of time and repetitive losing seasons, the Curse of the Billy Goat gradually became an urban legend in Chicago and part of baseball lore. Today, it is generally accepted that the Greek tavern owner placed a hex on the Chicago Cubs during the 1945 World Series that they would never again play in a World Series at Wrigley Field. And the curse seemingly remains intact after fifty-eight years.

William "Billy Goat" Sianis, died at home on October 22, 1970.[20] About his death, Chicago columnist and Pulitzer Prize-winning newspaperman Mike Royko commented: "It was typical of Billy Goat that he would die during the only five hours of the day when his place wasn't open for business. That's how good a businessman he was."[21] More than thirty years after Billy Goat Sianis' death, one wonders if he could have imagined that the Chicago Cubs would still not have won a National League pennant—or that his Curse of the Billy Goat would gain international recognition.

Whether Sianis intended it or not, he and his goat became part of the Cubs' lore and part of the folklore of Chicago itself. His Billy Goat Tavern became a Chicago landmark, made even more famous by the *Saturday Night Live* "Olympia Restaurant" comic routine featuring "Dan Aykroyd as short-order cook, Loraine Newman as unsmiling waitress, Bill Murray as happy-go-lucky counterman, and John Belushi as the boss who delights in letting people know exactly what they can and cannot eat."[22]

> Cheezborger
> Cheezborger
> No Fries, chips
> No Coke, Pepsi!
> (The Billy Goat Tavern original phrase was "No Pepsi, Coke." It is not known who changed the phrase in the sketch).[23]

The Billy Goat Tavern now boasts a chain of seven restaurants, and when you visit the tavern on lower Michigan Avenue you will still hear the counterman shout "Cheezborger, Cheezborger? Double cheese, that's the best."[24] The walls are covered with photographs and newspaper articles from Chicago's past. Clippings of newspaper articles telling the story of the Curse of the Billy Goat are scattered throughout the tavern, and ephemera on the walls documents the famous clientele who have imbibed there over the years.

Despite the fact that the Curse of the Billy Goat was eventually lifted by William Sianis in 1969—and several times since by his nephew, Sam Sianis, who now owns the Billy Goat Tavern (including once on the *Tonight Show* with Jay Leno)—many people insist that a remnant of the original double-whammy still exists.[25] The hex supposedly not only prevents the Cubs from winning a pennant, but also prevents them from winning a World Championship because they cannot reach the World Series. Each time the Cubs fail to reach the World Series, the hex is blamed.

Today, the Billy Goat Curse has found a permanent place in baseball lore as one of the most famous sports curses of all time, and it is inextricably intertwined with the history of the Chicago Cubs.

2

TINKER TO EVERS TO CHANCE

To appreciate the fate that has befallen the Chicago Cubs, it is important to recognize that the club was not always seen as a perennial loser. Indeed, the Cubs were publicly considered a powerhouse during the early years of the baseball league. This is a considerable difference from the so-called cursed team that can't win a pennant and has not won a World Series Championship since 1908—the longest drought of winning a World Championship among all professional teams.[1]

The Chicago Cubs' roots go back to 1876, when they became "one of eight charter members of the National League."[2] Originally playing under the nickname of the "White Stockings," the team went on to "win the inaugural National League championship."[3] Winning the first league championship was a somewhat auspicious beginning for a fledgling baseball team that would be destined, it seems, after 1945 to be perennial losers. After the turn of the century, around 1902, the Chicago team began to be referred to as the Cubs, and the club adopted the nickname as its moniker in 1907.[4] The previous year, 1906, the team set the "all-time major league record for wins in a season (116) and winning percentage (.763) en route to their first pennant of the 20th century" playing the Chicago White Sox in the 1906 World Series.[5] It was the only time that both teams from Chicago played in a World Series, with the White Sox prevailing four games to two to win the World Championship. The next year, the Cubs beat the Detroit Tigers four games to two to win the 1907 World Series Championship. In 1908, the Cubs followed up the previous year's success by beating the Tigers for the second straight year, becoming the first team in baseball history to repeat as World Series Champions.

"And the double-play combination of Joe Tinker, Johnny Evers and Frank Chance was on its way to baseball immortality, inspiring a 'sad lexicon' written by Franklin Pierce:"

> These are the saddest of possible words ... Tinker to Evers to Chance ... A trio of bear Cubs and fleeter than birds ... Tinker to Evers to Chance ... Ruthlessly pricking our gonfalon bubble ... Making a Giant hit into a double ... Words that are weighty with nothing but trouble ... Tinker to Evers to Chance.[6]

The Cubs failed to reach the World Series in 1909 but returned to the Series in 1910, losing to the Philadelphia Athletics. Nevertheless, the Cubs over a five-year span had appeared in four World Series, winning two and losing two and earning accolades throughout the country as an impressive and respected ball club. Nobody at the time could have realized or expected that the Chicago Cubs, ninety-five years later, still would not have won another World Series Championship.

The Cubs failed to win the pennant in 1911, but finished in second place, 7 1/2 games behind the New York Giants. For the next two years, the Cubs remained in contention, finishing each year in third place in the league. Still, it was clear that the New York Giants had replaced the Cubs as the dominant team in the league during these years. For the next four seasons, the Cubs were no longer a competitive team. That quickly changed in 1918, when the Cubs once again made it to the World Series. In order to draw larger crowds at home games during the World Series, the Cubs used Comiskey Park rather than Weeghman Park (renamed Wrigley Field in 1926 in honor of team owner William Wrigley Jr.) to host the World Series games played in Chicago.[7] The Red Sox went on to win the World Series four games to two.

During the 1918 Series between the Cubs and the Red Sox, Babe Ruth, who played primarily as a pitcher, threw a complete game and a shutout in the first game, winning the close contest 1-0. Ruth was also the winning pitcher in game four of the series, lasting eight innings before being replaced in the ninth by Joe Bush. He finished the series with seventeen complete innings and an impressive 1.06 ERA. Nevertheless, Ruth's performance in the series was matched, if not exceeded, by Boston's Carl Mays, who also won two games and completed the eighteen innings he pitched with a 1.00 ERA. Ironically, Cubs pitchers Hippo Vaughn and Lefty Tyler were equally as impressive as Ruth and Mays—each of the Cubs' four losses were by a mere run.

The following year, in December 1919, Boston sold Babe Ruth to the New York Yankees. The Red Sox, who won the inaugural World Series in 1903 and won five total World Series Championships by 1918, have yet to win another World Series Championship, despite having played in four Series since that time. Boston's eighty-five-year drought of World Series Championships is the third longest in baseball history. Only the eighty-six-year drought of the Chicago White Sox and the ninety-five-year famine of the Chicago Cubs are longer. Meanwhile, the New York Yankees and Babe Ruth made it to the World Series seven times over the next fourteen years, winning four World Series Championships. And the New York Yankee franchise went on to become the most heralded in baseball history. Like the fall of the Chicago Cubs, the fall of the Boston Red Sox from powerhouse to perennial loser is often blamed on a hex—"The Curse of the Bambino"—for selling Babe Ruth, arguably the best home run hitter in baseball history.[8]

The Cubs played mediocre baseball for the first five years of the 1920s. A fourth-place finish in 1923 was the team's best result for the first half of the decade. Two years later, in 1925, the Cubs began the second half of the 1920s in forgettable fashion by finishing in last place, 27 1/2 games behind the league-leading Pittsburgh Pirates. Nonetheless, the following year, William Wrigley Jr., who had purchased the Cubs in 1921, hired Joe McCarthy to manage the team, and the club immediately improved upon its last-place finish the year before. In both 1926 and 1927, the team finished in fourth place in the National League, but the Cubs were clearly getting better under

McCarthy's leadership. While the nation's stock market was about to crash in 1929, the Cubs' stock was on the rise—outpacing the Pittsburgh Pirates by 10 1/2 games to win the National League pennant. On October 8, 1929, the Cubs hosted the first World Series game ever to be played at Wrigley Field, losing to the Philadelphia A's by a score of 3-1 before a crowd of over fifty thousand. The following day, the Cubs were soundly beaten 9-3 before the fans at Wrigley Field. The Series moved to Philadelphia, and the A's went on to beat the Cubs four games to one to win the World Series Championship.

Despite the 1929 World Series loss, the Cubs, for the next nine seasons, enjoyed success similar to their past powerhouse teams of the early 1900s. Although they failed to win a World Series Championship in the 1930s, the club regained much of its earlier prominence by winning the National League pennant three times during the decade. The 1932 Cubs outpaced the Pittsburgh Pirates to win the National League pennant; however, in the World Series the team ran into a Yankee juggernaut that featured baseball greats Babe Ruth and Lou Gehrig. The Cubs were quickly defeated by the Yankees in four straight games. For the next two years, 1933 and 1934, the Cubs competed for the pennant but finished third in the standings both years. By the end of the following year, Chicago was again at the top of the National League. Nonetheless, the Cubs lost yet another World Series—losing to the Detroit Tigers four games to two.

Chicago battled the New York Giants for first place in the National League the next two seasons. Yet, the Cubs could not wrest the pennant away from New York, finishing second in the race both years. The next summer the Cubs overcame both the Pittsburgh Pirates and the New York Giants to win their fourth pennant in nine years. They went on to face the powerful New York Yankees in the 1938 World Series. Although it was a hard-fought series and each game was close, in the end the Cubs once again lost to the Yankees in four straight games. Following their defeat in the 1938 World Series, the Cubs' success during the 1930s was somewhat overshadowed by bad play when the team, once again, played mediocre baseball over the next six seasons. From 1939 to 1944 the Cubs finished no higher than fourth place in the league standings.

After finishing thirty games out of first place during 1943 and 1944, the Cubs shocked the baseball world by winning the National League pennant in 1945. However, the club lost a hard-fought World Series to the Detroit Tigers four games to three. It was during this contest that, according to baseball lore, the Curse of the Billy Goat was born when William Sianis and his pet goat were ejected from Wrigley Field.

Some people believe that the Chicago Cubs' failure to win a World Series Championship in their last seven attempts is not the result of being outplayed by the opposing American League team or based on the Cubs not playing up to their on-field abilities. Instead, they suggest that the Chicago Cubs suffer from a curse much like the Boston Red Sox, who have not won a World Series since the team's owner traded Babe Ruth to the New York Yankees in 1919.[9]

In comparison to the Red Sox, the Chicago Cubs have played in seven World Series since their last World Championship in 1908, the last in 1945, and lost them all. This feat was matched only by the Brooklyn Dodgers, who finally managed to beat the New York Yankees in the 1955 World Series to end their streak.[10]

Since the Curse of the Billy Goat has its beginnings with the 1945 World Series, the goat hex obviously had nothing whatsoever to do with the Cubs' World Series losses prior to that year. Some curse theorists believe that the Cubs' World Series misfortunes are due to the "Curse of Fred Merkle."[11] They point to an event that occurred during a game at the Polo Grounds between the New York Giants and the Chicago Cubs in September 1908 as the source of the Cubs' World Series flops. The Giants and the Cubs were locked in a tight, three-way pennant race that included the Pittsburgh Pirates. New York led Chicago by three games and Pittsburgh by 3 1/2 games when the Cubs played the Giants at the Polo Grounds on September 23, 1908. In the bottom of the ninth, with two outs, nineteen-year-old Fred Merkle, who was making his first start, was at bat. Merkle hit the ball into right field for a single, advancing Moose McCormick to third base. Al Bridwell was the next Giants batter to come to the plate. On the first pitch, Bridwell "pasted a neat but not gaudy single to center."[12] McCormick crossed home plate to seemingly win the game, "but Merkle, who was at first base, ran half way down to second, then turned, and hothoofed for the clubhouse"— a common practice in the league at the time.[13]

Almost immediately, hundreds of New York fans rushed onto the field in celebration of the apparent 2-1 victory. Nonetheless, the Cubs' Johnny Evers noticed that Merkle did not touch second base and called for the ball from the outfield to get a force out of Merkle at second, which would disallow the winning run. According to one account, Cubs third base coach, Joe McGinnity, saw what Evers was attempting to do and "grabbed the ball" before it reached Evers.[14] A brouhaha between the Cubs and Giants broke out on the field as McGinnity reportedly threw the ball into the stands. One of the Giants allegedly went after Merkle and brought him back to touch the second base bag. Of course, the Cubs later denied that Merkle came back onto the field and touched the base. Meanwhile, the Cubs retrieved the ball, either from the stands or somewhere else, and Evers got umpire Bob Emslie's attention before touching second base. Umpire Hank O'Day refused to make a decision on the spot but did later that night, ruling that Merkle was out at second and declaring the game to be a tie. The following day, September 24, 1908, the *Chicago Tribune*'s article by Charles Dryden commented:

> Minor league brains lost the Giants today's game after they had cleanly and fairly won by a score of 2 to 1. In the ninth round Merkle did a bone-head base running stunt identical with the recent exhibition which Mr. Gill, also a minor leaguer, gave at Pittsburgh three weeks ago.

Fred Merkle was unjustly given the pejorative nickname "Bonehead."[15] The label and the events of that day in September 1908 would torment Merkle his entire life. Ironically, Fred Merkle did nothing more than what was common practice at the time for a game-winning hit. In fact, earlier in the season a similar incident occurred when the Pirates beat the Cubs on a game-winning hit in the ninth inning.[16] Although Evers' quick thinking to force out Merkle may have saved the Cubs the game on a technicality, it went somewhat against the spirit of the game.

The Cubs finished the remaining games of the season with only two losses, the Giants lost five, and the two teams ended up tied at the end of the season. A one-game playoff was held in New York for the league championship. The Cubs won. They went on to beat the Detroit Tigers four games to one game in the World Series, becoming the first team in baseball history to win back-to-back World Series Championships.

Some curse theorists believe that the Cubs' failure to win another World Series is due to what they did to Fred Merkle in 1908, providing the basis of the little-known and so-called "Curse of Fred Merkle." [17]

For the rest of his baseball career, which lasted sixteen years, Fred Merkle went on to play with the Giants, Brooklyn Dodgers, Chicago Cubs, and New York Yankees. He played in five World Series in his career but lost them all. Merkle was forever haunted by the events of September 23, 1908. Before his death he reportedly commented, "I suppose when I die, they'll put on my tombstone, 'Here Lies Bonehead Merkle.'"[18] Today, many people believe that Fred Merkle was unjustly blamed for a "bonehead" play in September 1908, which cost the Giants the National League pennant and enabled the Cubs to march onward to their second consecutive World Series Championship. About the Fred Merkle incident, Keith Olbermann wrote the following:

> I have done a report of some kind on the Fred Merkle story, whether in print, on radio, or on TV, on or about its anniversary, September 23, virtually every year since I was in college. The saga has always seemed to me to be a microcosm not just of baseball, nor of celebrity, but of life. The rules sometimes change while

you're playing the game. Those you trust to tell you the changes often don't bother to. That for which history still mocks you, would have gone unnoticed if you had done it a year or a month or a day before. That's who Fred Merkle is. I have often proposed September 23 as a national day of amnesty, in Fred Merkle's memory.[19]

The irony is that the Cubs won a pennant in 1908 due to a minor technicality in the rules rather than winning the league outright. While they went on to win the World Series Championship, the club has not won another World Series since 1908. This is the basis for the belief by some people that the Cubs' inability to win a World Series Championship in their last seven appearances is due to the Curse of Fred Merkle.

3

THE CURSE YEARS

The first stage in the Chicago Cubs' transformation from pennant challenger to perennial loser began after the 1945 World Series, coinciding with Billy Goat Sianis' pronouncement that the team would never win another National League pennant. From 1910 to 1945, the Cubs won seven pennants. The only teams to win more National League pennants during this period were the New York Giants with ten and the St. Louis Cardinals with eight.[1] Since 1945, the Cubs have not won another National League pennant—the longest drought without a pennant in baseball history.

A year after their World Series loss to the Detroit Tigers in 1945, Charlie Grimm's 1946 Cubs finished in third place in the National League race. At the end of that baseball season, nobody blamed the team's failure to win the pennant on the Greek tavern owner's curse or any other hex. Nevertheless, the club's long downward spiral had begun. Starting in 1947 and continuing for the next twenty years, the Cubs—a club that at the time boasted ten National League pennants and World Series appearances and two World Championships since 1903—went from being a yearly pennant challenger to the annual doormat of the National League.[2] The Cubs played abysmal baseball—finishing near the bottom in the National League pennant race every year during this period and dead last in the league five times. The Curse of the Billy Goat gained Chicago urban legend status as the Cubs started losing year after year.[3]

Not much was reported in the newspapers about the so-called curse on the Cubs; however, back-to-back last-place finishes in 1948 and 1949 apparently made some people believers in the Curse of the

Billy Goat. One apparent believer was Philip Knight Wrigley, who became the owner of the Chicago Cubs when his father, gum mogul William Wrigley Jr., passed away in 1932.[4]

Facing the possibility of another last-place finish, P. K. Wrigley sent a letter to Billy Goat Sianis in September 1950 in an attempt to lift the Curse of the Billy Goat. "Will you please extend to (the goat) my most sincere and abject apologies as well as those of the Chicago National League Ball Club for whatever it was that happened in the past, and ask him to not only remove the 'Hex' but to reverse the flow and start pulling for us," pleaded Wrigley.[5] Sianis was not ready to remove the Billy Goat Curse, however.[6] In fact, when Sianis later moved his tavern to Michigan Avenue across from the Wrigley Building and was told he could not raise a Greek flag on the plaza, Billy Goat swore out another hex. "The Greek Flag will fly from your plaza before another pennant flies at Wrigley field," wrote Sianis in a letter to the Cubs. And so was born the little-known "Greek Flag Curse," overshadowed for decades by its more famous cousin, the Curse of the Billy Goat.[7]

Wrigley's effort to have Sianis change the Cubs' fortune did not work, and the club's fifth-place finish in 1952 proved to be the team's best finish in the National League standings throughout the 1950s.

In 1960, Charlie "Jolly Cholly" Grimm, the Cubs' manager for the 1945 World Series who had been replaced by Frankie Frisch, "the Fordham Flash," fifty games into the 1949 season, once again managed the Chicago Cubs. He lasted seventeen games, compiling a miserable 6-11 record before being replaced by Lou Boudreau. Still, neither manager made much of a difference in 1960. The Cubs finished in seventh place, thirty-five games out of first place that year. In the off-season, on December 20, 1960, team owner P. K. Wrigley instituted a "College of Coaches" approach, designed to have multiple coaches provide leadership, rather than the traditional, single-manager approach.[8] The intent was to "standardize instruction throughout the Cubs organization."[9] The new approach called for eight coaches to "rotate throughout the Cubs system, from Class D up to Wrigley

Field."[10] The experiment was unsuccessful and resulted in confusion throughout the organization. Contrary to Wrigley's hopes, this method of team management made it difficult, if not impossible, for the Cubs to become a consistent winner. Indeed, the Cubs played so poorly at times that the power of the Billy Goat Curse, even if real and accepted, could not have had an impact because there was little, if any, chance of the Cubs winning a pennant during these years.

In 1962, the National League expanded to ten teams with the inclusion of the Houston Colt 45's, later called the Houston Astros, and the New York Mets. The additional teams did little to aid the Cubs' chances to rise from the cellar of the National League. That year the Cubs lost 103 games, the most losses in a single year in the club's history, and finished in ninth place, 42 1/2 games out of first place and behind the newly formed Houston team.[11] An additional insult to the Cubs was the fact that Houston's manager, Harry "Wildfire" Craft, had managed the Cubs for sixteen games the year before.

Leo "the Lip" Durocher took over as manager of the Cubs in 1966, but the club once again lost 103 games, finishing in last place.[12]

William Sianis, who had moved his tavern to a new building on Michigan Avenue in 1964, added an addition in 1967 called the "'Wall of Fame' containing pictures of Billy's friends," which included many of the local newspapermen of Chicago.[13] William Granger of the *Chicago Tribune*, on December 26, 1967, wrote an article about the tavern's most recent addition and retold the story of the Curse of the Billy Goat:

> Once he was denied entry into the 1945 world series at Wrigley Field because of the goat. But Billy got even by putting a hex on the Cubs.
>
> The Cubs lost that world series and their fortunes plummeted after the war. Finally, Philip K. Wrigley, the owner, asked him to take the hex off. Sianis agreed. It did not seem to help the Cubs until recently.

Whether Sianis actually agreed to lift the Curse of the Billy Goat before December 1967 is not known.[14] If so, it was the first of many efforts by the Sianis family to end the hex.

The postwar Chicago Cubs, from 1946 to 1966, represent the worst teams in the club's well-known history. Of course, curse theorists claim that the Cubs' bad play was due to the Curse of the Billy Goat or some other hex. Others understandably have a difficult, if not impossible, time believing that the so-called Curse of the Billy Goat exists or that it has had any effect whatsoever on the outcome of the Chicago Cubs' games. Instead, inept management and poor player development and retention are often blamed for the Cubs' woes.[15] Nonetheless, the Chicago Cubs' mystifying yearly disappointments since 1945 have encouraged the mystique of the Curse of the Billy Goat to grow and thrive.

4

THE BIG HURT

For more than two decades after Billy Goat Sianis placed his curse on the Cubs—whether they were cursed or simply playing badly or being outplayed—Chicago still had not won another pennant. The Cubs' misfortune seemingly was about to change in 1969, when Chicago started the season with a 12-1 record and sole possession of first place. But the team's late-season collapse, resulting in a second-place finish in 1969, forever haunts the Cubs and is the epitome of the anguish that Chicago Cubs fans have endured since 1945.

The National League, which had expanded seven years earlier to ten teams, was split into two divisions in 1969—the Eastern Division and the Western Division. The Eastern Division consisted of the Chicago Cubs, Montreal Expos, New York Mets, Pittsburgh Pirates, and St. Louis Cardinals. The Western Division was composed of the Atlanta Braves, Cincinnati Reds, Houston Astros, Los Angeles Dodgers, San Diego Padres, and San Francisco Giants. No longer would the National League team with the best overall record win the pennant and go on to represent the National League in the World Series. Instead, the division champions would have a playoff for the National League pennant and the right to go on to play against the American League Champion in the World Series.

Ernie Banks, known as "Mr. Cub," Chicago's leading player and future Hall of Fame inductee who had signed with the Cubs sixteen years earlier, optimistically predicted the Cubs would win the pennant.[1] However, sportswriters did not share Banks' outlook concerning the Cubs' chances in 1969. Instead, the St. Louis Cardinals, the defending National League Champions, were again picked to win the pennant.

Although the Cubs were expected to be competitive in 1969, one sportswriter predicted that the "Cardinals will break Cubs fans' hearts again."[2]

On April 7, 1969, President Richard Nixon "officially opened the 1969 season by throwing out the first ball in the game between the Senators and Yankees."[3] The Chicago Cubs' opening game with the Philadelphia Phillies was set for the following day. On Wednesday, April 8, 1969, *Chicago Sun-Times* sportswriter Edward Munzel threw out the first ball to start the Cubs' season, and Ernie Banks began his seventeenth "hunt for a National League pennant."[4] A record crowd of 40,796 watched the Cubs win their first game when, in the eleventh inning, Willie Smith hit a pinch-hit home run to win the game 7-6.[5]

Over the next six games the Cubs improved their record to 6-1 on the season. By April 14, 1969, the team was in sole possession of first place in the division with a one-game lead over the Pittsburgh Pirates. The following day, the *Chicago Tribune*'s David Condon announced that Billy Goat Sianis was officially lifting the so-called Curse of the Billy Goat:

> The 1969 CUBS have done better than excite all of Chicagoland. They also have healed the hiatus between Messrs. Philip Knight Wrigley and Billy Goat Sianis, those renowned Michigan boulevard restaurateurs.
>
> Mr. Wrigley, owner of the Cubs, sought to patch up the differences way back in 1950.
>
> But Billy Goat waited until yesterday to make the truce official. Yesterday he dispatched Wrigley a letter seeking to reserve four seats for the Cubs' 1969 world series matches. . . .[6]

Chicago continued its winning ways, and on April 19, 1969, the club won its sixth game in a row, beating the Expos in the eleventh inning 6-5. Chicago was seemingly unbeatable with a 10-1 record and alone in first place. Nevertheless, the Pirates, since being beaten twice by the Cubs a week earlier, had kept pace with Chicago and were still only two games behind the Cubs.

The city of Chicago was ecstatic about the early performance of the Cubs, but the city was also pleased with the Chicago White Sox, who were in first place in the American League Central Division. "Is this 'Next Year?' Sox, Cubs in First," read the headline in the *Chicago Tribune*'s sports page.[7] A year earlier, the two Chicago baseball teams were both in last place in their respective leagues. Fans now expected the Cubs to finally win the pennant and play in the World Series. Yet, despite their hot start at the beginning the season, the Cubs began to lose more frequently. On May 9, the *Chicago Tribune* noted that the Cubs were 11-1 up to April 20 and were 8-9 since that time, but they still had a two-game lead on Pittsburgh.

In mid-May, the Chicago Cubs, now leading the division by five games, flew to Houston for a three-game series with the Astros. The *Tribune* noted that the Cubs didn't like the Astrodome because the team had a 19-44 losing record when playing in the dome. The Curse of the Billy Goat was not blamed for the Cubs' misfortunes in Houston, however. Instead, the *Tribune* claimed that there was a so-called "Dome Hex" on Chicago.[8] The newspaper recalled that the Cubs were in first place the previous year when they lost four straight games in the dome, and after those losses the Cubs never played well again. In actuality, the writer was referring to the 1967 Cubs, who two seasons earlier came to Houston only a half game behind St. Louis and lost four straight to the Astros. In any event, after the Cubs beat the Astros on May 16, 1969, the *Tribune* commented that Chicago had snapped the Astros' "jinx."[9]

Chicagoans now fully expected the Cubbies to win their division, win the National League pennant, and bring home their first World Series Championship since 1945. *Tribune* writer David Condon, impressed by how the Cubs were playing, wrote the following:

FOR THE GOOD of baseball, let's break up those wreckers from Wrigley Field, the Chicago Cubs, before they make a farce of the national pastime. If the Cubs maintain their current pace, they figure to win their division crown by about 22 games. Then, of course, they'd win the playoff and finally whip the American league champions, 4-0, in the world series.[10]

Meanwhile, Billy Goat Sianis, the man who placed the Curse of the Billy Goat on the Cubs in 1945 and who finally lifted the hex in April 1969, was going to Ireland with the Chicago Police Sergeants' Association. Sianis was an honorary member who wore the badge 007 (Goat, Billy Goat!).[11] With Chicago playing strong baseball, the goat hex supposedly lifted, and its originator heading to Ireland, was there anything to stop the Cubs' march to the pennant? Even opposing managers like Harry "the hat" Walker of the Houston Astros were convinced that the Chicago Cubs were too strong. "I just can't see how this team is going to fold. The Cubs have not one but three pitchers [Fergie Jenkins, Ken Holtzman, and Bill Hands] who are stoppers, who will keep them from going into any prolonged losing streaks."[12] Although Walker did not see any weakness in the Chicago Cubs, he acknowledged that in the past a few teams had been overtaken late in the season.

But the Cubs' long ride at the top of the Eastern Division standings, with a lead now at 8 1/2 games, had created mass hysteria in Chicago. The frenzy surrounding the team started to become a distraction. The left field fans known as the "Bleacher Bums," who wore hard hats, began receiving a great deal of attention in the press.[13] When a Cincinnati player hit a home run into the section, one of the Bleacher Bums threw the ball back onto the field, and the section began chanting: "We don't want it! We don't want it!"[14] The rowdy and boisterous fans in the section had routines and songs that they would sing during the games. Later in the season, opposing players and the media would complain about the Bleacher Bums' behavior. At one point, Curt Flood, an outfielder for the St. Louis Cardinals, complained that the crowd was throwing steel ball bearings at him.[15] Lou Brock, who was a Cub before being traded in 1964, complained about the crowd and the media. "You have glorified them and they show their gratitude by behaving like that. It's not right!" Brock exclaimed.[16] In one game, a Bleacher Bum extended his helmet over the wall into the playing field to catch a possible home run ball hit by a Cub, but Lou Brock managed to catch the ball anyway. After the game, it was reported that the umpire would have ruled the Cubs batter out due to fan interference if Brock had not made the play.[17]

Adding to the excitement of the pennant race, the *Chicago Tribune* announced that Ernie Banks would start to write a daily column for the newspaper, chronicling the remainder of the season. "Banks, the most exciting and colorful player among the Cubs as they streak hopefully toward their first National League Championship since 1945, will start his daily series in Sunday's TRIBUNE."[18] Banks assured readers that his views would be "through rose colored glasses" and that he would keep a positive spin in his articles.[19] The Cubs held a nine-game lead over the New York Mets when Banks started his daily column on June 15, 1969.

It was a joyous time in Cubville. But the exciting season was not without distractions for the team. Leo Durocher married Lynne Walker Goldblatt on June 19, 1969.[20] Over two hundred guests—including Mr. and Mrs. Philip Knight Wrigley and their son Bill, and most of the Cubs family—attended the three-minute ceremony and gala event at the Ambassador West Hotel. The ceremony started twelve minutes late and ended so quickly that Cubs stars Ernie Banks and Billy Williams, and their wives, missed the nuptials.[21] Still, the wedding reception apparently had little effect on the Cubs; they beat the Expos 2-0 the next day.

It began to seem inevitable that the Chicago Cubs would maintain their first-place lead in the Eastern Division. *Tribune* writer Robert Markus, who at the start of the season had picked St. Louis to win the division, now told readers that he was "throwing in the towel."[22] Markus proclaimed, "Neither Pittsburgh nor New York is a sound enough club to win a pennant."[23] The catchy phrase "Cub

Power" was being used by Chicagoans to describe the first-place team as it raced toward its first pennant in twenty-four years.[24] "Cub Power" pennants, posters, and bumper stickers were being sold throughout the city. Meanwhile, radio stations were playing the 1969 Cubs' theme song, "Hey, Hey! Holy Mackerel," and vendors were selling for $1.25 each the popular record.[25]

The hysteria of the 1969 Chicago Cubs seemingly had taken on a life of its own. Rather than keeping their focus on upcoming games, Cubs players decided to set up an autograph booth for each home game.[26] The booth was placed under the third base grandstand behind the Cubs dugout and was to be open from 12:15 p.m. to 12:45 p.m. each day. Before each home game, rather than being allowed to go about their normal game day routine, three different Cubs players signed autographs for eager fans. A signing schedule was even printed in the *Tribune*.[27] It was an unprecedented move at Wrigley Field—and likely an unnecessary distraction for a team fighting to hold on to first place and trying to win its first pennant since 1945.

Another distraction occurred on July 26, when Chicago fans learned that the Cubs' Manager, Leo Durocher, had left the ballpark in the third inning of the game to spend three days at Camp Ojibwa in Eagle River, Wisconsin, where his new bride's twelve-year-old son was attending school, for a parents' reception.[28] The news caused a stir in Chicago, and team owner P. K. Wrigley was reportedly upset with Durocher for leaving the team. He declared that Durocher's departure during a tight race and a close game was like a ship trying to steer itself without a rudder.[29] Wrigley was concerned that the players, who were hustling to try to win the club's first pennant since 1945, might conclude from Durocher's actions that he was not as dedicated to winning the National League title.

Journalist Robert Markus came to Durocher's defense. "The Cubs, thanks to Durocher, are winners now and would win the pennant with Zsa Zsa Gabor at the helm," wrote Markus.[30] The Durocher debate caused some distraction but quickly subsided over the next seven games. It appeared that the Cubs were, indeed, headed for the playoffs. "Orators and authors were formulating plans to follow the

Cubs in the National League playoffs, and then to the world series," the *Tribune* commented.[31]

There were even more distractions as some players cashed in early on the team's success by doing commercial endorsements for things like underwear sales and other outside activities.

The ballyhoo and hysteria that surrounded the Cubs throughout the season later came back to haunt the team. When the team began to lose more frequently, columnist Edward Prell wondered if the Cubs were "feeling the strain of the pennant race."[32] Prell noted, "The Cubs have been under some strange phenomenon at home, losing 10 of their last 13 before bumper crowds in Wrigley field."[33] The most reasonable explanation for the Cubs' losses during this time was that the team was simply being outplayed at home. Possibly, the off-field distractions had caused the team to lose its focus. Nevertheless, nobody at the time, at least publicly, was proclaiming the so-called Curse of the Billy Goat to be responsible for the Cubs' woes.

Still in first place by 2 1/2 games, the Cubs traveled to New York for a pivotal two-game series against the Mets. New York won the first game 3-2. The next night, just as the Cubs' Don Kessinger was getting ready to lead off the game against the Mets' Tom Seaver, a black cat suddenly appeared on the field:

> It sprinted to the batter's box, stopped and stared at the next batter [Ron Santo] and headed for the visitor's dugout. There it raised its furrowed tail, hissed at Durocher and then scurried back beneath the stands.[34]

The Cubs went on to lose the second game against the Mets by a score of 7-1. And the black cat, thereafter, would forever be another part of Cubs lore, with some fans later blaming the animal for what was in store for the team. The Mets had swept the series, extending the Cubs' losing streak to six, and had closed to within a half game of first place. The next day, the Philadelphia Phillies limited the Cubs to three hits to beat them 6-2, and the Mets beat the Expos twice. "Mets In First! Cubs Lose 7th Straight," stunned Chicagoans would read the next day.[35] New York had finally chased down and passed the Chicago Cubs, who had been in first place for one hundred and fifty-six days. Chicago lost its eighth straight game the next day. Meanwhile, the Mets were in the middle of their own streak—an eight-game winning streak that would not end until New York had won fourteen in a row. Despite having nineteen games left to play, Chicago's 1969 pennant race was essentially over—finishing twenty days later, on October 2, 1969, eight games behind New York for second place in the Eastern Division.

The 1969 Chicago Cubs, "the best team that never won," are now remembered for their late-season collapse in the summer of '69.[36] Players and fans had different explanations for the collapse.

Ernie Banks later stated that the Cubs' late-season collapse was due, in large part, to the fear of losing:

> A lot of people say we needed more rest, the bench, the black cat in New York, all of that, but it wasn't pressure or outside activities or anything like that.
>
> It was fear. When you haven't won, it's scary, and that's life. Dealing with the uncertainties, the unknown, it's fearful when you get there facing the unknown. And that's what I think happened to us in 1969.[37]

The team simply did not have any experience in leading the league for such a long period of time. Toward the end of the season, rather than going out each day to play to win, the Cubs went out each day to play not to lose. And that was even more the case when the Cubs went to the West Coast in late August. "The Mets were at home. Every night when we went to the ballpark the Mets' score was posted. We'd look up at the scoreboard and we'd be thinking, 'We've got to win now.' It was the same thing night after night."[38] But Cubs pitcher Bill Hands later was more direct and to the point. "We had so much pressure on us that we folded. It's that simple."[39]

Fans ascribed Chicago's September fold to a number of different causes, and some people even blamed the Curse of the Billy Goat for the team's collapse. Nonetheless, Billy Goat Sianis, the father of the double-whammy itself, told David Condon and others at the Billy Goat Tavern that the Cubs' demise was not due to the curse:

> Some people say the Cubs ran out of gas. Some blame Durocher. Some say they spent too much time singing about holy mackerel [the 1969 theme song]. Others say the Cubs were too busy selling underwear ... Some say it was the Bleacher Bums. Some say it was the Billy Goat hex. Yes, for many years my Billy Goat hex cost the Cubs pennants. When the Billy Goat hex is on you, there is nothing except trouble.
>
> I removed the Billy Goat hex from the Cubs. So that is not why they blew the pennant....
>
> The reason the Cubs lost the division championship is very simple. I explain it without innuendo or rumor or anything else. The whole thing in a shellhole is: The Cubs lost because the New York Mets just played like hell! [40]

Some people blamed the black cat for causing the Cubs' downfall when it jinxed the team by running onto the field during the critical two-game series against the Mets in New York during September. Yet, the Cubs had started to fold long before the black cat's appearance in New York—Chicago went into the two-game series having lost thirteen of its last twenty-three games. The Cubs' 9 1/2-game lead over the Mets evaporated to a 2 1/2-game margin during the same period. After losing the two games to the Mets, the Cubs finished the last twenty games of the season with a miserable 8-12 record. No, it appears the black cat had little, if anything, to do with the Cubs' demise in the summer of 1969.

Of the various explanations and theories, Sianis' reasoning seems the most probable. Truly, the Mets "played like hell" to take the division crown.[41] New York won thirty-six of its last forty-seven games, for a blistering .706 winning percentage to close out the season.

While the 1969 Chicago Cubs' collapse is a source of great anguish to both former players and fans, the late-season flop is neither the only one of its kind nor the most devastating collapse in baseball history. Indeed, that dubious distinction goes to the 1964 Philadelphia Phillies, who lost a 6 1/2-game lead over the Cincinnati Reds with only twelve games left to be played, when they lost ten straight games.[42] Moreover, the Cubs' 9 1/2-game slip from first place is not the largest margin blown by a baseball team.[43] The California Angels lost an eleven-game lead in 1995, and the Houston Astros blew a 10 1/2-game lead in 1979.[44] Two other teams, the 1978 Boston Red Sox and the 1993 San Francisco Giants, "allowed a 10-game lead to slip through their hands."[45]

It is widely believed that the Cubs, whether they needed rest or had too many distractions or simply folded under the pressure of the season, lost the division crown and a chance for their first pennant in twenty-four years by simply not finishing the season playing as well as they had started it. On the other hand, the Mets helped themselves by playing better baseball toward the end of the season, and they won the division title going away.

Either way, in the end, Cubs fans, once again, would have to "Wait till next year!"

5

WAIT TILL NEXT YEAR

The Chicago Cubs were picked to place second in their division in 1970 and began the new season with high expectations. Ferguson Jenkins, who won twenty-one games for the Cubs the year before, started the first game of the year on the road against the Philadelphia Phillies. Jenkins lost 2-0 and the Cubs immediately dropped a game behind the Phillies and the Mets. Chicagoans wondered whether the Cubs were over their previous September's collapse, which had cost the team its first National League pennant in twenty-four years. The fans themselves were having a difficult time forgetting—Chicago radio stations were playing the 1969 Cubs' theme song, "Hey, Hey! Holy Mackerel" as the season started.[1] "It only serves to remind me of a year I would just as soon forget," one fan complained.[2] But Leo Durocher reassured Chicagoans that the Cubs were ready to play ball: "Last year is as old as yesterday's newspaper."[3]

On April 14, 1970, the Cubs began a ten-game homestand at Wrigley Field before 36,316 people.[4] The fans watched as Chicago beat the Phillies 5-4. After the game, a brouhaha erupted on the field between unruly fans and ushers trying to maintain order. Thereafter, the Cubs management requested more police support for Wrigley Field. Over the next nine days, Chicago went on an amazing, nine-game winning streak to remain unbeaten at home, taking control of first place by 2 1/2 games over St. Louis and Pittsburgh.

For the next two months, the Cubs, as they had done the year before, led the Eastern Division race—extending their lead over second place by as many as five games during mid-June. Yet, that all changed starting on June 21, 1970, as the team lost twelve straight games in nine days and quickly dropped to second place, 2 1/2 games behind the New York Mets. Still, the Cubs stayed within a few games of first place the remainder of the year and even closed the gap to within half a game in early September. The team could not regain possession of first place, however. They finished the season on October 2, second in the standings and only five games behind the division champion Pittsburgh Pirates. This was closer to a first place finish than the year before. Nevertheless, the team's June collapse, like the '69 Cubs' September fold, seemingly cost them the division crown and a chance for a National League pennant. Again, Cubs fans had to "Wait Till Next Year" for a chance to win another pennant.

The next season saw the Cubbies playing poorly and being beaten often. It was not until mid-May that the team managed to compile a winning record. They ended the season fourth in the standings but never really put up much of a challenge for the division title. Next year had come and gone.

In 1972, the Cubs' season started in much the same way as it had the year before. On May 21, 1972, Chicago was 15-15, nine games out of first place.

Chicagoans were unable to explain the Cubs' consecutive collapses in 1969 and 1970 and the team's poor play since those seasons. The Curse of the Billy Goat became a convenient way to justify Chicago's failure to win a National League pennant since 1945, even though Billy Goat Sianis had supposedly lifted the goat hex in 1969. David Condon remarked, "Cubs' Hex Lingers On," and proceeded to retell the history of the Billy Goat Curse and the Chicago Cubs' pennant drought since 1945:

> ENTER THE GOAT! Jolly Cholly Grimm's Cubs were happy to escape Detroit. . . .
>
> Happy fans greeted the happy warriors' train at Union Station. One of the merriest fans was William [Billy Goat] Sianis, keeper of a saloon and a prominent herd of goats. Billy had unique intentions.

Gov. Dwight Green was in Wrigley Field the next afternoon. Mayor Ed Kelly [Dick hasn't always had the job] was present, too. Mr. Billy Goat Sianis and his blue-ribbon goat, Sonovia, also appeared.

Mr. Sianis presented a pair of box seat tickets and escorted Sonovia to choice pews. The Frain ushers started squawking on those new fangled handy-talkies and very quickly both goats, Billy and Sonovia, were being rushed exitwise. Sonovia's ticket was retrieved. Presently it is mounted in the Billy Goat Inn, more prominent than pictures of the many Pulitzer Prize winners who patronize Billy Goat's Chicago Club North.

When the Tigers surged ahead by winning the fourth and fifth games, Billy Goat placed an eternal hex on the Cubs. As an afterthought, he telegraphed owner Philip K. Wrigley: "Who Smells Now?" ...

A quarter century, plus, has elapsed. The series since has visited sites not even in the majors in 1945: Milwaukee, Baltimore, Los Angeles, San Francisco, Minnesota, the miracle Mets' Shea Stadium. But it hasn't returned to Wrigley Field.

Billy Goat's hex reaches out from the grave.[5]

David Condon often visited the Billy Goat Tavern, and his two articles in 1969 about Billy Goat Sianis and the goat hex began the transformation of the Curse of the Billy Goat from a Chicago urban legend to a widely known curse in baseball lore. Condon's article on the goat hex in May 1972 further ingrained the Cubs' curse within the baseball community and the psyche of Cubs fans. And although Condon had noted that Billy Goat Sianis had lifted the curse in 1969, he now maintained that the Curse of the Billy Goat was an "eternal hex" that was still in effect. Not that the contradiction mattered much—the name of Sianis' pet goat had changed from Murphy to Sonovia in the three-year span as well.[6]

The Cubs ended the 1972 season in second place without really contending for the division title, finishing eleven games behind league-leading Pittsburgh. It was the third time in five years that the Cubs had finished in second, and Chicagoans still felt that something was missing—a National League pennant. But Cubs fans always had next year, right?

The '73 Chicago Cubs won their first two games of the season but lost the next three. Nevertheless, the team slowly began to play more consistently and battled to take sole possession of first place by May 1. Throughout much of the month of May, Chicago clung to its first-place standing by a slim margin. Toward the end of the month, the Cubs extended their margin to 4 1/2 games over New York. Despite a six-week run in first place, Cubs fans had not yet caught the dread pennant fever—an occurrence that was not missed by the *Tribune*'s Robert Markus: "Looks like Cub fans are maturing right along with their team. Nobody seems to be very excited about the club's big lead in the National League East. Memories of 1969, I guess."[7] Instead, it was White Sox fans who were starting to talk about winning the pennant. Like the Cubs, the White Sox were in first place, having held on to the lead for more than a month and a half. "The southsiders are almost a cinch to win the American League's Western Division. Possibly the pennant, too," proclaimed the *Tribune*'s Robert Markus.[8] Still, Cubs fans did not let the recent success of the White Sox alarm them. "Because, of course, as great as the White Sox are, you know they can't beat the Cubs in the world series," one fan insisted.[9] Considering the Cubs had not won a pennant since 1945, and had not won a World Series since 1908, the fan's prediction of a World Series victory over the White Sox was fairly audacious. But then, the Chicago White Sox hadn't exactly been burning up the bases over the years either—one pennant in fifty-three years is hardly awe inspiring.[10]

On June 19, 1973, the White Sox lost 3-1 to the California Angels, and their run of fifty-two straight days at the top of their division was over.[11] The team regained the lead the next day with a 5-3 victory over the Pittsburgh Pirates, but over the next few games the club slid to third place in the standings. This caused the *Tribune*'s Bob Logan to remark that the "south side epidemic of pennant fever was abating."[12] Meanwhile, the Cubs had an 8 1/2-game lead, and the south siders' symptoms of optimism shifted back to the north siders.

> And just like it was back in the good old days—1969—the Friendly Confines of Wrigley Field are being transformed into an outdoor insane asylum. Glazed eyeballs and coated tongues are unmistakable symptoms of the dread "flag flu" and a good share of the 32, 328 customers appeared to be coming down with a bad case.... THERE IS NO known cure for this malady.
>
> In short, be careful walking under bridges around Sept. 30 in case the Cubs blow it again .... Of course, a growing body of observers now think that the Cubbies' yearly el foldo is a thing of the past.[13]

Some Chicagoans, mindful of the usual collapse of the Cubs, now believed that the Curse of the Billy Goat would strike at any time, as it supposedly had before, to prevent the Cubs from winning their first pennant since 1945. Visitors at the Billy Goat Tavern, including "the young secretaries, Bunnies, and Social Registerites who take their lunch in the place," began taunting Sam Sianis, who inherited the Billy Goat Tavern from his uncle, the late Billy Goat Sianis, to lift the curse.[14] "Go on, take off the hex on the Cubs. You can break Billy Goat's will," they pleaded.[15] But Sam remained steadfast, "the double-whammy will last forever," he responded.[16] Nevertheless, on July 3, 1973, both the Chicago Cubs and the Chicago White Sox were in first place, and the possibility of a Chicago World Series and the economic impact it would bring to Chicago enticed Sam Sianis to lift the Curse of the Billy Goat. Sam therefore went to Wrigley Field and purchased two box seats for the game scheduled for July 4 between the Cubs and the Phillies. The night before the game, Sam painted a sign for his goat Socrates to wear. The sign read: "All Is Forgiven. Let Me Lead You To The Pennant. Your Friend, Billy Goat."[17]

The following day at noon, "Sam donned a Cubs' cap. He put a Cubs' cap on Socrates, and affixed the signs to the pet."[18] A huge limousine from Fabulous Howard's Limousine Service transported Sam and the goat to Wrigley Field. A red carpet was rolled out and Socrates proceeded to the gate. But the ushers were reportedly given strict orders "that tickets or not, Sam Sianis was not going to take his goat into the holy ball park."[19] Sam refused to be denied so easily and stubbornly led the goat around the block, but "was refused at each entrance."[20] No refund would be given either. "But Sam and Socrates, the goat, were welcomed into Ray's Bleachers [a bar on Sheffield Ave.]—home of the revered Bleacher Bums—and given refreshments."[21] And the Cubs went on to beat the Phillies 3-2.

David Condon of the *Tribune* forewarned Chicagoans that the Cubs management may have cost the team another pennant: "THE CUBS HAD their golden opportunity to cast out the devil on July 4. But thanks to the cavalier attitude of the Cubs' vice-presidential think tank, they blew it big. So the hex still holds. The North Siders probably have kissed the pennant goodbye again. Just like every season since 1945."[22] Condon was no longer the only journalist in Chicago reporting on the so-called hex. David Israel of the *Chicago Daily News* also reported the goat incident in the press, noting that the most recent goat suffered the same indignity as did its forebear in 1945.[23] Moreover, Israel commented that Sam Sianis had forewarned the Cubs to be nice to the goat or the goat hex would be built up.

Condon's prediction of doom might have been quickly forgotten but for the Cubs' collapse that began the day after Sam Sianis and the goat were barred from Wrigley Field. At the time of the 1973 goat rebuff, the Cubs were in first place, 8 1/2 games ahead of their nearest rival. Over the next twenty games, the Cubbies only managed to win four games and they surrendered first place almost without a fight. Then Chicago slipped to fourth place—losing eleven straight games at one point—winning only five of their next twenty games and causing some people to believe that the Curse of the Billy Goat had struck again.

Of course, many people place no weight in superstitions or baseball curses. The practical explanation for the Cubs' misfortune is that the club, for whatever reason, either played poorly or was outplayed throughout much of the remainder of the season. Still, the 1973 team's losing play started almost immediately after Sam Sianis and his pet goat Socrates were barred from entering Wrigley Field, justifying curse theorists' connection between the two events. While the team's collapse following the '73 goat incident likely is a mere coincidence—another in a long line of strange happenstances—when a team like the Cubs has not won a pennant since 1945, it's hard to blame fans for seeking an explanation elsewhere for the Cubbies' yearly "el foldo."

Beginning in 1974 and for the next nine seasons, the Cubs returned to being a mediocre team. Whatever stability that the club had attained in the Durocher era (1966-1972) was gone. In the years after Durocher, nine different managers guided the Cubs. In some seasons, the team quickly faded following opening day and were never in a serious challenge for the division crown. Other years, the Cubbies merely pretended to play the role of a title contender—managing to battle for control of first place by some time in May, but always yielding the lead after a slump. One example of the type of seasonal collapse that often occurred during this period happened during the 1977 season. On May 28, 1977, the Cubs managed to wrest first place from the Pirates with a 6-3 victory.[24] A month later the Cubbies were in sole possession of first place with a record of 47-22 and an 8 1/2-game lead over St. Louis. Throughout the month of July, the Cubs held on to first place, but their lead slowly began to diminish. By August 6, the Pirates shared first place with the Cubs.[25] However, Chicago proceeded to lose seven of its next ten games, including five in a row at one point, and the season was essentially over. They finished in fourth place, twenty games behind the division champion, with an 81-81 record. Ironically, the team's 81 wins and .500 overall season record was the best finish Chicago could manage from 1974 to 1983.

On June 16, 1981, the sports world was somewhat surprised when the Tribune Co., in the middle of a fifty-day baseball strike, bought the Chicago Cubs from William Wrigley for 20.5 million dollars.[26] Estate and inheritance taxes of 40 million dollars were largely the reason that Wrigley sold the team.[27] It was a good deal for the Tribune Co., which also owned WGN Television, which in turn held the broadcast rights to the Cubs games. On hearing the news of the change in ownership, President Ronald Reagan commented: "It's an end of an era, but hopefully the beginning of another era."[28] Reagan, an Illinois native, had become a fan years earlier while broadcasting Cubs games for WHO in Des Moines.[29] The sale was welcomed by fans who hoped that the Tribune would put "new life into the Cubs" and would "develop a good farm system rather than fill the roster with high priced free agents."[30] More importantly, many people believed that the Tribune Co. had the resources to make the Cubs a better ball club and the desire to do so—a desire that the Wrigley family, with the exception of William Wrigley Jr., who died in 1932, apparently lacked.[31]

The Cubs finished the first half of the 1981 strike season in last place in the Eastern Division with a record of 15-37. After the Tribune Co. bought the Cubs, the team improved somewhat in the second half of the season. Nevertheless, the Cubs' new ownership signaled that changes would be made for the next season. Manager Joey Amalfitano was replaced by Lee Elia, and the team began to play somewhat better but still finished in fifth place in the division. The following season, the Cubs made little in the way of improvement, and Elia was replaced after one hundred and twenty-three games. Charlie Fox took Elia's place for the final thirty-nine games of the season. However, the team finished in fifth place and nineteen games behind the division winner for the second year in a row.

Fans once again had to "wait till next year" for the miracle season they wished for.

6

THE MIRACLE SEASON

The Cubs hired Jim Frey as manager for the upcoming 1984 season.[1] The change brought with it a renewed hope among fans that the Cubbies' prospects for the future might improve. One journalist even thought the Chicago Cubs were "ripe for a 'miracle' season."[2] Nevertheless, it's likely that many people thought the preseason prediction was foolhardy considering Chicago's dismal performance the previous summer and the club's general ineptitude over the past ten years. This is not to mention the team's inability to win a pennant since 1945 or even a division title since the National League split into two divisions in 1969.

The Cubs opened play on the road against the San Francisco Giants and started the 1984 season on a positive note when Ron Cey hit a home run in the ninth inning for a 5-3 victory. It was a "rare opening day triumph" for the Cubs, and the occasion was not overlooked by the *Chicago Tribune*: "Quick, cut out the national league standings, Cub Fans. Your team is in first. You can look it up."[3] Still, not everyone was ready to hop on the Cubs' bandwagon just yet. "Cubs manager Jim Frey almost swallowed his tobacco chaw when asked if he had to begin guarding against complacency on this would-be National League East juggernaut," the *Tribune* mused.[4] The Cubs won their second game of the season two days later but suffered the team's first loss the following day. Once the two-game winning streak was ended, some people feared that the team would quickly return to their losing ways. "Things are beginning to seem distressingly familiar for the Cubs," remarked the *Tribune*'s Fred Mitchell.[5] A few days later, the Cubs returned from their West Coast road trip with a 3-4 record and already were three games behind the first place New York Mets.

Back in Chicago, Wrigley Field had a new look due to a number of off-season changes. The Torco Oil sign that usually "sported drawings of players" was "draped in basic black and yellow."[6] The scoreboard had new "spiffy tic-tac-toe green outlines," and the clubhouse was newly renovated.[7] The home opener brought changes to the team's lineup as well. The Cubs started Leon Durham at first base instead of long-time crowd favorite Bill Buckner. Chants of "Buckner, Buckner" were heard at times during the day from the crowd of 33,436, along with a chorus of boos when Durham was at bat.[8] One fan at Wrigley Field was Billy Goat Tavern owner Sam Sianis, who brought his pet goat Socrates.[9] The Cubs management apparently was now willing to try anything for a chance at a winning season and invited Sam and the goat to enter Wrigley Field for the home opener.

On Friday the Thirteenth, with a billy goat allowed in the stadium for the first time since the fourth game of the 1945 World Series, Steve Trout "tossed a complete game to end the surprise Mets' six-game winning streak" by a score of 11-2.[10] The Cubs followed up on the home-opener success with two more victories, moving them to within one game of first place. Although not acknowledging whether he believed the goat hex had been lifted or not, journalist Bernie Lincicome was impressed with the Cubs' turnaround following the home opener:

> The Cubs are playing with a dash unfamiliar to Wrigley Field .... The Cubs may become patsies again, but for now, they are nobody's hand towel.[11]

The Cubs continued their new winning ways and, with a record of 10-6, took over possession of first place on April 25, 1984.[12] The team's rise to the top of the Eastern Division was not overlooked by baseball fans throughout the United States. In the nation's Capital, Republican Congressional Representative Elwood Hillis of Indiana made the following comment before Congress about the rising baseball powerhouse: "Tuesday night, at 11:07 p.m., Washington time, the Chicago Cubs defeated the St. Louis Cardinals 3-2 and moved into sole possession of first place in the National League's Eastern Division."[13] Hillis was more circumspect after the Cubs' loss the following night when he observed, "Glory has always been a brief and fleeting thing for the Cubs."[14] More to the point, Hillis remarked that "The lovable losers of Wrigley Field ... always find ways to snatch defeat from the jaws of victory."[15] Still, Chicago rebounded a few days later, beating the Pittsburgh Pirates 2-1 to regain first place with a 12-8 record.[16]

Throughout most of May 1984, the Cubs held on to first place by a slim margin. Ticket sales in Chicago were up by 250,000 from the year before, and the club was on pace to break its all-time single-season attendance record of 1,670,993 set in 1969.[17] "Unless one of the disasters not unknown to the North Side falls on the team," commented the *Tribune*.[18]

Some thought that the 1984 Cubs were "possibly the best hitting club" that Chicago had seen since the 1970s.[19] Moreover, the team seemingly had good overall speed, a strong defense, a strong bench, and good starting pitching. Still, wary of the Cubs' previous disappointments, one writer reminded fans that "three times in the last 15 seasons," the Cubs had faded down the stretch.[20] And, almost as if on cue, the Cubs' two-game margin was erased at the end of May, and the club fell to second place. The team responded well, though, regaining first place two days later. In early June, it was rumored that *Sports Illustrated* was planning to put the Cubs on the front cover of its next issue. "Normally, that's a jinx," one writer remarked. "But how do you jinx a team that has won one pennant since the invasion of Normandy?"[21] A few days later, on June 11, 1984, the *Sports Illustrated* hit the newsstands featuring Leon Durham on the cover.[22]

Throughout June and July 1984, the Cubs continued to battle for first place. By early August, the team was clinging to a slim, 1 1/2-game lead over the Mets. Chicagoans were not yet hopping on the bandwagon, however. The *Chicago Tribune* expressed this sentiment with an editorial picture proclaiming a 1984 World Series win for the

Cubs accompanied by a caption that read: "No, not yet ... Hey, This is the Cubs! They could still blow it!"[23] Nevertheless, the Cubs continued to remain in first place and, after sweeping the Mets in a four-game series in early August, they found themselves up by 4 1/2 games.[24] By mid-August, the Cubs' margin was a slim 1 1/2 games. Chicago remained focused, though, and extended its first-place lead to six games by the end of August. With nineteen games left in the season for both teams, the Cubbies still had thirteen games remaining at home. With a record of 45-23 at Wrigley Field, they had the best home record in baseball.[25]

As the Cubs closed in on their first division crown, recollections of late-season collapses by other Cubs teams began appearing in the newspapers. Even the dread black cat from the 1969 season was, once again, brought up as a topic. "WITH EACH NEW day, it seems the ugly vestiges of the 1969 season are being exorcised by the spirited Cubs of 1984," noted the *Tribune*.[26] The newspapers weren't talking about the Curse of the Billy Goat, however. "The dog has come and gone in Wrigley Field. The choking dog that generations of Cub fans were convinced would leap from the throats of the 1984 Cubs is nowhere in sight. The dog has come and gone," proclaimed Steve Daley of the *Chicago Tribune*.[27]

On September 24, Rick Sutcliffe's 4-1 victory over the Pirates won the Cubs their first National League Eastern Division title.[28] "The burden of a franchise and a proud city were lifted as the Cubs scratched the 39 year itch that had represented the organization's scarlet letter," one writer exclaimed.[29] Manager Jim Frey was exuberant, remarking, "We got the monkey off our back."[30] "For seven months, all the Cubs had been hearing was about how the Cubs folded in 1969."[31]

Chicago finished the season a few days later with the best overall record in the National League. The club's record on the road was its best since 1945, and its home record was the team's best since 1936.[32] Nevertheless, the National League pennant was no longer given to the team with the best record at the end of the regular season as it was in 1945. Instead, the Cubs had to play a best-of-five-game series against the Padres to reach the World Series.

On October 2, 1984, Wrigley Field was packed with excited fans eager to see the Cubbies defeat the Padres, and Sam Sianis and his pet goat were invited to Wrigley Field.[33] Ernie Banks threw out the game ball and the Cubs, with Rick Sutcliffe pitching, proceeded to pound San Diego 13-0 to take a one-game lead in the series. The next day, Steve Trout pitched a five hitter for a 4-2 victory over the Padres. One win away from their first National League pennant and World Series appearance since 1945, the Cubs headed to San Diego, without the goat, for the third (and possibly final) game of the series. The Padres proceeded to rip Dennis Eckersley, winning by a score of 7-1. Still, most people viewed the loss as a momentary delay for the Cubs; after all, many thought the Cubbies were on their way to their first World Series since 1945. Yet, when the Padres' Steve Garvey slammed a home run in the ninth inning the next day, winning the fourth game by a score of 7-5, the division series was tied. The next night, the Cubs surrendered four runs in the seventh inning and lost the division series to the Padres. A ground ball that slipped through Leon Durham's legs forever haunts Cubs fans as a reminder of the 1984 postseason collapse.

Unlike the division title victory celebration a week earlier when Chicago fans spilled into the streets in Pittsburgh, "Wrigleyville saloons emptied quickly."[34] The Cubs' three straight losses in San Diego were attributed by some journalists as a matter of choking—nothing more, nothing less. Sam Sianis later recalled the 1984 season. "That was the first time they invited me to the game," referring to the Cubs' first postseason game since 1945. When the Cubs went to San Diego with a two-game lead, Sianis observed, "They left me behind and they lost."[35] The Billy Goat Curse, however, was not blamed for the playoff collapse, at least not publicly and not at the time. Later, though, with fans unable to explain the unexplainable, the Curse of the Billy Goat was suspected of claiming yet another victim—the 1984 Cubs.

Some fans, at least those who believe in the curse, do not consider that there are several other reasons why the Padres beat the Cubs three straight times to win the National League Eastern Division title in 1984. Although the Cubs did have a better overall record than the Padres in 1984, the difference between the two clubs was marginal at best.[36] The Cubs and the Padres split the twelve games they played during the regular season—showing how even the two teams actually were as they headed for their postseason showdown.[37] The Cubs won their only two games of the series playing at home, where they had the best winning percentage in the major leagues. Nonetheless, the Padres had a somewhat comparable winning record at home.[38] Given the two teams' records, it should not have come as a shock when San Diego beat the Cubs three straight times at home to win the league championship series and proceed to the World Series.

From the inception of the five-game National League Championship Series format in 1969 until 1984, the Cubs were the only team in the National League to lose a league championship series after leading 2-0. They're also the only team in the National League during that time to win the first two games of the league championship series. Still, the Cubs' feat of losing three straight games and a league championship series after leading the series by two games is one that had been accomplished before. In 1982, the California Angels beat the Milwaukee Brewers in the first two games of the American League Championship Series.[39] The Brewers went on to beat the Angels in the next three games to win the American League pennant. Of course, the fact that the Angels folded with a 2-0 lead in a league championship series two years before the Cubs' collapse offers little consolation to Cubs fans who still feel the pain of the fall of 1984.

In 1984, fifteen years after the late-season collapse of the Cubs in the summer of 1969 and forty-nine years after the Cubbies had played in the postseason, the general malaise felt yearly by fans was somewhat eased with the team's first Eastern Division title. The curse seemingly had been lifted at the start of the season, Chicago overcame its habit of folding late in the summer, and the Cubs appeared to be a headed for their first National League pennant and World Series appearance since 1945. But the Cubs' fate took a different path when Chicago found a new way to lose—a postseason collapse.

To many people, the Curse of the Billy Goat was very much alive.

Chicago Tribune File Photograph

William "Billy Goat" Sianis and his pet goat Murphy at the ticket turnstile at Wrigley Field.

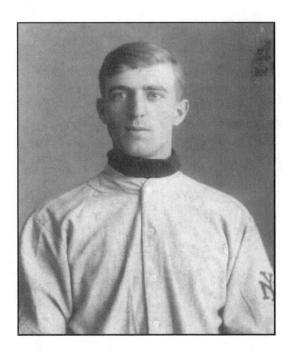

Fred Merkle was unjustly blamed for not running to second base on a game-winning hit against the Cubs on September 23, 1908. The Cubs ended up beating the New York Giants in a one-game playoff and went on to win the 1908 World Series. The play would haunt Merkle for the rest of his life, and some people believe that the Curse of Fred Merkle prevents the Chicago Cubs from winning another World Series Championship.

Photographs 45

Chicago Tribune File Photograph

The ticket that William Sianis tried to use for his pet goat Murphy during game four of the 1945 World Series. The ticket hangs on the wall of the famous Billy Goat Tavern in Chicago.

—*TIMES Photo*

This goat had seat—
This goat causes uproar in Wrigley field yesterday, but is permitted to stay put in box seat after owner, "Billy Goat" Sianis, tavern owner, protests animals being given bum's rush by ushers.

Chicago Daily Times File Photograph

William "Billy Goat" Sianis and his pet goat Murphy were permitted temporarily to stay in the box seat section at Wrigley Field before eventually being ejected from the stadium. Reprinted with special permission from the *Chicago Sun-Times*, Inc. 2004. "This goat had seat." October 7, 1945.

Photographs

Chicago Daily Times File Photograph

William "Billy Goat" Sianis and his pet goat Murphy made it into Wrigley Field despite the initial efforts of ushers. Reprinted with special permission from the *Chicago Sun-Times*, Inc. 2004. "Getting whose goat?" October 6, 1945.

Photographs

Chicago Sun-Times Photograph by Phil Velasquez

Sam Sianis and goat were allowed into Wrigley Field for the Cubs home opening game in 1984. Reprinted with special permission from the *Chicago Sun-Times*, Inc. 2004. Sam Sianis takes mascot to field. Photograph by Phil Velasquez, April 14, 1984.

Chicago Tribune File Photograph

Sam Sianis and goat were invited into Wrigley Field to stop the Cubs record-setting twelve-consecutive-game, home losing streak in 1994.

The walls of the Billy Goat Tavern are filled with things from Chicago's past, including the ticket William "Billy Goat" Sianis tried to use to get his goat a seat for the fourth game of the 1945 World Series.

7

THE BOYS OF ZIMMER

After winning their first Eastern Division title in 1984 and appearing in the postseason for the first time since 1945, the Cubs in 1985 tried to build upon their newly achieved success. For a time, it looked like the magic of the 1984 Cubs was carrying over. The Cubs were 7-1 after beginning the 1985 season with an eight-game homestand. Despite the fantastic start, they were tied for first with the New York Mets. By June 11, 1985, however, the Cubbies had built up a four-game lead on the Mets and were in sole possession of first place in the Eastern Division. Starting the next day, though, thirteen straight losses, including four to the Mets, ended the Cubs' hopes of repeating as division champion.[1] Even so, consecutive playoff appearances for the Chicago Cubs were not exactly the norm—the last time the team accomplished the feat was in 1908.

Over the next three years, the Cubs would not finish a season with a winning record. Jim Frey was replaced after racking up a 23-33 record to start the 1986 season. Coach John Vukovich took over his duties for two games before Gene Michael took over the reins of the Cubs. Still, the managerial change made little difference as the Cubs finished in fifth place in the division and thirty-seven games out of first place. The following year, the team won six games more than the previous year but still ended the season in last place. Don Zimmer was hired to manage the Cubs in 1988. The team made some improvement on the field and even began playing under lights at Wrigley Field on August 8, 1988, but still finished in fourth place at the end of the year.[2]

Entering the 1989 season, little was expected from the "Boys of Zimmer," who finished in the standings twenty-four games behind the division-leading Mets the previous year. The Cubs started the 1989 baseball season at home before 33,361 fans on April 4, 1989.[3] Once again, Wrigley Field had undergone a great deal of renovation in the off-season. Sixty-seven new luxury skyboxes were added to the mezzanine level, a press box was constructed behind home plate, and a food court was added in the upper deck. The luxury boxes added to the comfort of corporate sponsors at Wrigley Field, but some fans complained that the skyboxes cut off their view of the playing field.[4] One of the fans reportedly at Wrigley Field that opening day was Sam Sianis with his pet goat, which last made an appearance at the stadium in 1984—the last time the Cubs won the Eastern Division title. The Cubs beat the Philadelphia Phillies in the season opener.

Throughout much of the season, the St. Louis Cardinals, Montreal Expos, and Chicago Cubs battled for first place in the Eastern Division. But the Cubs wrested first place from the other teams and slowly began to pull away. By June 22, 1989, the Cubs were in first place with a three-game lead. However, Chicago went on to lose seven straight games and fell behind Montreal by 2 1/2 games. Meanwhile, Cubs fans were filling seats at a local theatre to see a play called "Bleacher Bums," which portrayed life as a Chicago Cubs fan.[5]

Slowly the Cubs again began to gain ground on the lead. By August 17, 1989, they had regained first place and increased their lead over the New York Mets by 4 1/2 games. The Cubbies then, once again, went on a losing streak of six games but managed to retain first place and a game-and-a-half lead over the Mets. With ten games left, the Cubs had a three-game advantage over the second-place St. Louis Cardinals and a 5 1/2-game lead on the New York Mets. This time there would be no late-season collapse. The Cubs won eight of their last ten games and earned the best record in the National League, winning their second division title in five years.

The Cubs were scheduled to face the San Francisco Giants, winners of the Western Division, in the National League Championship Series (now a seven game series). The last time the two clubs faced one another in a game with a pennant on the line was October 1908—in a one-game playoff that was necessary due to the infamous Merkle play. One journalist commented that "Merkle's retribution could be at hand" with a Giants' pennant.[6] Another wondered whether Chicago would lose a sense of itself should the Cubs win the pennant.[7]

The first two games of the National League Championship Series were scheduled to be played in Chicago. A postseason lottery for seven thousand tickets was held. Ticket scalpers inflated prices for the games, and vendors were selling T-shirts with "The Boys of Zimmer" printed on them. These items and anything else with the Cubs name on it sold like hotcakes.

On October 4, 1989, the Cubs-Giants National League Championship Series began. In the bottom of the first inning, the Giants jumped to a three-run lead. However, the Cubs responded in the bottom of the inning with two runs of their own. But Will Clark's two home runs helped San Francisco to overpower the Cubs 11-3. The following day, the Cubs scored six runs in the bottom of the first and coasted to a 9-5 victory to even the series.

The Cubs headed to San Francisco for three more games. The "season to remember" quickly turned sour as the team lost the championship series (a best-of-seven-game series) and the pennant to the San Francisco Giants.[8] The loss was heartbreaking to Cubs fans, but the team's quick exit (4-1) kept the pain felt by fans from reaching the level of the 1984 Cubs' collapse.

The usual Cubs jokes and cynicism surfaced following the latest postseason loss. However, little about the hex was mentioned in the newspapers following the 1989 defeat in the National League Championship Series, despite the Curse of the Billy Goat having already achieved the status of an urban legend in Chicago. Instead, some fans wrote to columnist Mike Royko claiming that his comments about San Francisco fans stirred them from complacency, and the fans blamed Royko for the three straight losses to the Giants.[9]

Despite winning the Eastern Division title and finishing with the best overall record in the National League twice in the previous five years, the Cubs ended the 1980s without a league championship pennant or an appearance in the World Series. This extended the team's World Series drought to fifty-four years. Although the club had managed to overcome its seemingly annual, late-regular-season collapse *a la* the '69 Cubs, a new obstacle had emerged—the postseason collapse. The decade of the 1990s, rather than symbolizing the Cubbies' resurgence as an annual challenger, epitomized the team's fall back to mediocrity.

8

LIFTING THE CURSE

The Chicago Cubs characteristically finished below .500 seven times during the 1990s. It was a feat matched or exceeded by the Cubbies in each of the four previous decades.[1] But the decade of the 1990s is best remembered for the Cubs' record-setting losing streaks of 1994 and 1997 and the club's public recognition of the Curse of the Billy Goat. The Cubs were the first major league franchise in history to formally acknowledge the existence of a baseball curse.

Tom Trebelhorn became the manager of the Chicago Cubs in 1994.[2] Almost immediately, his tenure as the team's leader seemed to be tenuous at best. The Cubs opened the 1994 season with three straight losses to the New York Mets at Wrigley Field. The club then went on an eight-game road trip, with its first stop in Montreal. In the Cubs' fourth game of the season, rookie pitcher Steve Trachsel won his first major league game and Tom Trebelhorn's first game as Chicago's manager, with a 4-0 victory. Several days later, the Cubs returned from their road trip with a losing record of 3-8. The team then proceeded to lose five more games at Wrigley Field, extending their home losing streak to eight games.

Still unable to win at home, the Cubs left the friendly confines of Wrigley Field for a seven-game road trip. Upon their return to Chicago a week later, with an overall record of 6-14, the Cubs dropped their next home game to the Colorado Rockies, pushing their home losing streak to nine games.[3] Meanwhile, the club was receiving unwanted national notoriety due to its ineptness at home, becoming the butt of nightly jokes by Jay Leno on the *Tonight Show* and other entertainment programs and sports shows.[4] The ridicule was so bad that some south siders, usually antagonistic toward their north side brethren, were sympathetic toward the Cubs' plight. After all, Sox fans were no strangers to negative exposure in the media.[5]

Unable to explain the Cubs' inability to win a game at Wrigley Field, Trebelhorn, for the first time in Cubs history, publicly blamed the Curse of the Billy Goat for the club's woes. The *Chicago Tribune*, on April 30, 1994, published the following comments:

> Manager Tom Trebelhorn has it figured out: It's the curse of the Billy Goat that has the Cubs off to a record-setting 0-9 start at Wrigley Field this year.

The story of the Curse of the Billy Goat was retold by the *Chicago Tribune*, and the hex, once again, was blamed for the Cubs' inability to win. "That goat's got to go. That's all there is to it," exclaimed Trebelhorn.[6] "I've got to go down to that tavern and talk to that guy about the goat.... We'll let the goat run the bases and water the outfield. We'll let him eat some grass and I'll kiss him. Whatever it takes."[7] According to Toni Ginnetti of the *Chicago Sun-Times*, Trebelhorn was even considering having Wrigley Field exorcised by a friend from Portland, Oregon, or possibly getting "[comedian and Cubs fan] Bill Murray or his friend [comedian] Father Guido Sarducci [played by Don Novello] to do it."[8]

The Cubs lost three more games, extending their record-setting, home-field losing streak to twelve games before help arrived to end the drought. On May 4, 1994, Sam Sianis and a billy goat arrived at Wrigley Field on a mission of mercy to stop the record-setting losing streak.[9] Former Cubs players, including Ernie Banks and Glenn Beckert, also were present to aid in any way they could.[10] Although the curse had been lifted before and a goat had made an appearance in 1984, Banks "didn't see any harm in trying again and personally led the goat around the outfield grass and past both dugouts before the first pitch."[11] According to Cubs second baseman Ryne Sandberg, the team was open to suggestions: "A lot of the guys didn't know the history of it, and they got a lesson. It was kind of fun."[12]

Steve Trachsel pitched seven solid innings, and Sammy Sosa and Eduardo Zambrano each hit home runs to end the losing streak at twelve games with a 5-2 victory over the Cincinnati Reds. After the game, "almost everyone—including Trebelhorn—was willing to give some credit to Banks and the Billy Goat."[13] Cubs first baseman Mark Grace thought Trachsel had more to do with the Cubs winning than anything but acknowledged that he wanted to keep the goat around, even if it looked ugly.[14] Trebelhorn thought the goat looked "maternal," not ugly: "It's very nice to have a maternal goat help you end a losing streak."[15] Nevertheless, the *Tribune* was quick to remind relieved Chicago fans that the Cubs still had "the worst record in the major leagues at 7-18."[16]

The home-field slump ended all hope that the Cubs would vie for the division crown, and the 1994 season mercifully ended early due to a baseball strike. The Cubs finished in last place in the Central Division with a 49-64 record. Steve Trachsel went on to have a good year and was a finalist for National League rookie-of-the-year. Yet, the sophomore jinx apparently affected Trachsel—he was the only Cub starting pitcher to have a losing record in 1995.[17] In fact, one reporter commented that Trachsel was a mere 3-28 at Wrigley Field after his first two years in the league.[18] Curse theorists began to blame Trachsel's poor performance at Wrigley Field on the Curse of the Billy Goat. According to the story, a minor incident occurred when Sam Sianis and the goat were brought to Wrigley Field to stop the twelve-game losing streak in 1994, and some people even claimed that Trachsel kicked the goat. At the time, Trachsel reportedly told *Sun-Times* writer Toni Ginnetti the following:

> I was upset when they brought him [the goat] by the bullpen when I was warming up. It was kind of a distraction. The goat was kind of in my way. It was more laughs for the fans than anyone else. If they believe that's the way it is, they should have him sit in the front row.[19]

About Steve Trachsel's apparent dislike of the goat's presence on the field, Ginnetti jokingly remarked, "Oh, no, not another goat affront."[20] Steve Trachsel later insisted, however, that the story had been twisted. "I didn't mind the goat. It was the cameramen and reporters that ticked me off," Trachsel recalled.[21] Presumably this will someday give rise to the little-known "Curse of the Cameramen and Reporters," right?

During the 1997 preseason, the Cubs publicly "authenticated the curse, going as far as to send marketing chief John McDonough and former Cub Ron Santo to a curse removing press conference at the Billy Goat Tavern."[22] Further endorsing the goat hex, the Cubs announced a television advertising campaign for Old Style Beer featuring a "curse of the goat" ad that was scheduled to run throughout the season.[23] The "Old Style TV commercial centered around a stuffed and mounted goat head, a replica of the goat once owned by the late William 'Billy Goat' Sianis."[24] Scheduled to debut Thursday, March 20, 1997, the commercial featured a goat that came to life and spoke to a Cubs fan, promising to lift the goat curse in exchange for a beer. Radio spots and outdoor advertising were also planned for the Old Style campaign.

The Cubs management had come a long way since the initial goat incident with Billy Goat Sianis in 1945 and the second rebuff in 1973 when it adamantly refused to allow Sam Sianis and his goat Socrates to enter Wrigley Field. After allowing Sianis and a goat into the stadium in 1984 and again in 1994, the higher echelon was now going out of its way before the season started to embrace the Curse of the Billy Goat, to pronounce the hex lifted, and to use the curse as a marketing ploy.

Mike Royko of the *Chicago Tribune* responded to the announcement of Old Style Beer's goat ad campaign with some thoughts about the Cubs' true problems over the years:

Lifting the Curse

It was Wrigley, not some goat, who cursed the Cubs.

It's about time that we stopped blaming the failing of the Cubs on a poor, dumb creature that is a billy goat. This has been going on for years, and it has reached the point where some people actually believe it. Now a beer company, the Cubs and Sam Sianis, who owns Billy Goat's Tavern and the accused goat, have banded together to lift the alleged curse that was placed on the Cubs in 1945—the last time they were in the World Series.[25]

Royko went on to blame P. K. Wrigley for the team's misfortunes, citing "a second-rate minor-league system," a failure to sign the best available black ballplayers, a team that got "older and more enfeebled" as "other teams quickly got better," and overall poor management in "running the worst franchise in baseball."[26] Royko reasoned that since 1981, when the Tribune Co. purchased the team from the Wrigley family, the Cubs simply "haven't been good enough" to make it to the World Series yet.[27] He concluded that the franchise's woes had nothing whatsoever to do with the Billy Goat hex, although some people were beginning to believe in the curse.

With the goat hex supposedly officially lifted one more time at a preseason press conference attended by Cubs officials, Chicago opened the 1997 baseball season on the road against the Marlins and the Braves. After losing three straight games to Florida, the Cubs traveled to Atlanta for a three-game series against the Braves. On April 4, 1997, the Cubs "blew a late lead" in game four and lost their fourth straight game of the season.[28] Starting 0-4 at the beginning of the season was the "worst for the Cubs since 1983, when they began the season with six straight losses."[29] But the lovable losers weren't done yet. The Cubs continued their losing ways in the next two games, extending their losing streak to six games.

Returning to Chicago with a record of 0-6, the Cubs already were considered by some to be a "lousy ballclub."[30] Despite the gloomy outlook, Cubs slugger Sammy Sosa predicted that the team would win its next game.[31] Sosa's prediction aside, given the team's bad start at the beginning of the season—its worst since 1983—some remained convinced that the Curse of the Billy Goat was still plaguing the Cubs. On opening day at Wrigley Field, some fans, eager to see the losing streak end, "paid $1 to get their pictures taken with a goat under a sign reading 'Lift the Curse.'"[32] Others tried a different method to defeat the curse—a morning show called in a witch to "cast a lucky spell on the Cubs."[33] But the efforts had no effect on the outcome of the game. Instead, the Cubbies lost their first game at Wrigley Field and the seventh straight game since the season started, tying the club's all-time record set in 1962. The following day, the "blue-and-white 'L' flag hung drearily above the centerfield scoreboard," signifying the Cubs had lost their eighth game in a row.[34] About the Cubs' 1997 record-setting losing streak, *Chicago Tribune* journalist Paul Sullivan made the following comments:

> They are known for their rich history of futility, but these Cubs are outdoing themselves.... This team is separating itself from all the other bad teams in the cursed history of the 121-year-old franchise.[35]

Fearing that they might go "0 for '97," the club's veterans called for a players-only meeting.[36] The private meeting had little effect out on the playing field, though, and the Cubs lost their eleventh straight game on April 15, 1997, surpassing the National League mark set by the Atlanta Braves.[37] Meanwhile, in an effort to break the losing streak, the Cubs' legendary announcer, Harry Caray, had made a pledge to sell beer at his Harry Caray Restaurant for 45 cents. After the Cubs lost their eleventh game, Caray sarcastically commented, "I'm going to go out of business."[38] Radio sportscaster David Kaplan pledged to continue to live in a van parked in the McDonald's parking lot across from Wrigley Field until the Cubs won.[39]

Andy MacPhail of the Cubs management asked for patience from the fans while answering questions at a meeting at a Broadcast

Advertising Club luncheon that had been scheduled before the season and before the losing streak began.[40] After answering a multitude of questions about the woes of the Cubs, one final question was presented for MacPhail to address: "What about the goat?"[41] Before MacPhail could answer, Caray shouted, "Shoot him," and the crowd exploded with laughter and applause.[42] Two days later, *Tribune* columnist Joe Knowles featured a picture of a billy goat in his column and wrote the following about the losing streak: "This whole losing streak is just part of your plan to put Harry Caray's place out of business, isn't it?"[43]

The Cubbies' 1997 losing streak had reached twelve games. Yet, unlike 1994 when Sam Sianis and a goat were brought in to finish off the drought, this time the goat was not called upon to end Chicago's misery. Instead, the Cubs lost their thirteenth straight game of the season on April 19, 1997, when they were beaten by the New York Mets by a score of 6-3.[44] The following day, Chicago lost the first game of a double-header, extending to fourteen games its record-setting number of losses to start the year.[45] Fortunately, Harry Caray's Restaurant was saved from serving 45-cent beers for the rest of the season and going out of business when the Cubs won the second game of the double-header.[46]

Although the Cubs managed to end their fourteen-game losing streak to start the season, their year was essentially over before the month of May began. Of course, the usual suspect for the Cubbies' on-field flops by this time was the Curse of the Billy Goat. And about the Cubs' latest fiasco, Paul Sullivan of the *Chicago Tribune* wondered: "Is it just an eerie coincidence that the first franchise to publicly acknowledge its curse—even spreading word of its history through a prominent ad campaign—already has broken club and National League records for all-time worst start of a season?"[47] "Eerie coincidence" or not, most people recognize that a team's failure to win a championship for a long time has more to do with "an incredible streak of poor management decisions and bad players" than a curse.[48] Nevertheless, McDonough acknowledged that the goat curse talk was likely to continue until the Cubs eventually won a pennant. "We'd just as soon close the book on [the curse]. But the only way to do that is by winning," said McDonough.[49] Finishing the 1997 campaign in last place with a record of 68-94, sixteen games behind first place, was not going to do much to help rid the Cubs of the Curse of the Billy Goat.

  The Cubs started out the next season in a better fashion, winning six of their first seven games. The team later finished the season in second place, 12 1/2 games out of first place, earning the club's first wild card bid for postseason play. However, the 1998 team proved to be no match against the Atlanta Braves, which had the league's best record. The Braves easily dispatched the Cubs in four straight games before losing to the San Diego Padres in the National League Championship Series.

  In 1999, the Cubs closed out the twentieth century in forgettable fashion. The lovable losers finished in last place, thirty games behind the division winner. This was the team's worst finish of the 1990s. But then, the Cubs aren't known for consecutive playoff appearances either. The last time the Cubs were in the postseason in back-to-back years was 1908—the last time the Cubs won the World Series.

9

YEAR OF THE GOAT

On Friday, November 15, 2002, Dusty Baker was hired to manage the Cubs in 2003 and to end the club's drought of World Series Championships since 1908.[1] Baker was well aware of the club's history of late-season collapses and that 1945 was the last time the team had won a National League pennant. Nonetheless, he placed little weight on the potential impact that history or the Curse of the Billy Goat would have on the Cubs' upcoming season, and he exhorted Cubs fans to avoid negative thinking and negative comments, which they seemed to express on a daily basis.[2]

Throughout the upcoming season, the team would be constantly reminded of both the Cubs' history and the fans' desire to win a World Championship. A billboard operated by the Lakeview Baseball Club was located on Sheffield Avenue and was visible from Wrigley Field. The large blue sign with white letters read: "AC145895." The cryptic meaning was clear to all Cubs fans—fourteen years since a Division Championship, fifty-eight years since a National League Championship, and ninety-five years since a World Championship. It took Baker the whole year to know what the numbers represented.[3] Still, many people in Chicago believed that Dusty Baker was the man, maybe the only man, who could turn the Cubs' woes and ninety-five-year drought around. He had some of the best credentials in baseball, having played nineteen seasons in the major leagues and having managed the San Francisco Giants for ten more.[4] During his time managing the Giants, Baker received the National League Manager of the Year Award three times, and his San Francisco Giants won the 2002 National League pennant before losing the World Series to the Anaheim Angels.

As American armed forces raced to Baghdad in soaring temperatures during the Iraqi War, the 2003 Cubs' campaign started on a "windy and chilly" day in New York, with a 15-2 win against the Mets.[5] The "Dusty Baker Era" had begun in a positive way, and despite the fact that the club had lost 95 games the year before, Cubs fans were excited about the team's prospects for the new season. Still, others were quick to remind Chicago fans that the season had only just begun: "It was only Opening Day, and it was only one victory, but the Cubs haven't had a lot of feel good days," one writer noted.[6] Almost on cue, the Cubbies lost their next game 4-1.

The Cubs went on a five-game winning streak in mid-April that catapulted them into first place in the division. Over the next four months, Chicago battled the St. Louis Cardinals and the Houston Astros for first place. Each team at times took a turn at the top of the division. In time, fans began to believe that this was finally the year the Cubs would win the World Series.

As the season progressed, several incidents occurred that had the potential to distract the team from playing its best. In June, during the first inning of a game against the Tampa Bay Devil Rays, Sammy Sosa's bat split, exposing a foreign substance—cork. He was ejected from the game.[7] Although the Cubs went on to win the contest by a score of 3-2, the prospect of losing Sosa to a league suspension, even for only a few games, took away any joy in Cubville. The national media began to question Sosa's previously untainted character and his credentials as a home run hitter. Sosa claimed that he had innocently and mistakenly used a bat intended only for use during batting practice, but he was suspended despite the claim.[8] "The Cubs went 3-4 but held on to first place in the NL Central while Sosa served a seven game suspension for using a corked bat."[9] Once the suspension was over, Sosa was razzed by some fans around the league about the cork incident, but the episode quickly faded as a hot topic of discussion in the media.[10]

A month later, more controversy and attention in the media was focused on the Cubs after Dusty Baker publicly commented that "Blacks fare better in hot weather than Whites do."[11] One writer commented that Baker's theory was just another excuse for the Cubs' seemingly annual collapse—"Too many day games, organizational cheapness, the Billy Goat Curse. Now you can add the 'Wilting White Man Theory' to the list."[12] But like Sosa's corked bat incident, Baker's "heat and skin color" opinion quickly went by the wayside. And the Cubs had other more immediate concerns to deal with anyhow. On July 7, Cubs center fielder Corey Patterson twisted his left knee and was lost for the season.[13]

With yet another problem to deal with during his first year as manager of the Cubs, Baker was asked if he now believed that the Cubs were jinxed. "No," he responded. "But I did go by the Billy Goat [Tavern] today to get a hamburger."[14] (He should have got a cheeseburger, everyone knows that cheeseburgers are the best!) The Cubs had to replace Patterson for the remainder of the season if they had any hopes of winning the division and marching toward their first World Series in ninety-five years. The list for a replacement was short—Baker wanted Kenny Lofton, who had made an indelible mark in baseball as an all-star while playing twelve years in the league, mainly with the Cleveland Indians.[15] The trade was desperately needed as the team was now three games out of first place and had fallen to a .500 record.[16] While the Cubs were patching one hole in their roster due to an injury, another hole emerged. Pitcher Mark Prior was knocked out of action when he collided with an opposing player on July 11, 2003.[17] Prior was finally able to pitch a game on August 5, winning a 3-0 decision over the San Diego Padres.

The Cubs started September with a five-game homestand against the division-leading St. Louis Cardinals, who held a 2 1/2-game margin on Chicago in the standings. In the first game of a doubleheader, the Cubs closed the Cardinals' gap by one game when they scored six runs in the fifth inning to win by a score of 7-0. After the night cap was rained out, the Cubbies won the rescheduled game the next afternoon when Sammy Sosa blasted a home run in the bottom of the fifteenth inning. But the team lost the following game by a score of 2-0 and remained 1 1/2 games out of first place.[18]

The next morning, around 9:45 a.m., Baker was reportedly seen "dusting" a substance over the infield and outfield at Wrigley Field.[19] When later asked about the substance by a journalist, who referred to it as "magic dust," Baker declined to identify the material but claimed that the ritual had something to do with the "force of good."[20] Whatever the so-called magic dust was, the ritual seemingly brought good luck to the home team as the Cubs went on to win the next two games—winning 4 of 5 games in the series with the Cardinals. A game later, the Cubs beat the Brewers to move into a tie for first place with the Houston Astros. During the game, Cubs reliever Antonio Alfonseca was ejected from the game after "belly bumping" an umpire while objecting to a call. Alfonseca was suspended by the league for seven games, but he filed an appeal and the suspension was later reduced to five games.[21]

Tired of the talk of past Cubs collapses in September, and after the team was "13 of 17 since Sept. 1, their best stretch of the season," Baker believed the team was entitled to rid itself of its "lovable loser" label.[22] Throughout most of September, Chicago battled the Astros for first place in the division.

In mid-September, some discussion began to take place on WGN's John Williams Radio Show about attempting to "Reverse the Curse" of the Billy Goat.[23] The plan entailed trying to get a goat into the Houston Astros' Minute Maid Stadium before the Astros played San Francisco. Fans reasoned that if the Astros denied the goat admission into the stadium, the curse may be reversed or, at least, transferred. Three listeners of the show decided to follow up on the idea, flying to Houston, renting an SUV, and buying a goat. On Monday, September 22, 2003, the three men led the goat, dubbed Virgil Homer, to the ticket takers at Minute Maid Stadium. With the incident being heard live on the John Williams Radio Show, the goat was not allowed into the stadium. For added measure, the men recited the following verse:

> Two years shy of 60 cursed,
> For all this time, the Cubs were the worst.

Armed with goat and mystic verse,
We hereby Reverse The Curse!

You had your chance to let him in,
But now no more will the Astros win.

We'll take our goat and leave this place,
Along with your hopes in this pennant race![24]

The Giants beat the Astros 6-3. The next day, on September 23, the Cubbies regained first place with a one-game lead over the Astros.[25] *Chicago Tribune* journalist Phil Rogers later commented: "Suddenly the Cubs seem above Jinxes. Perhaps those WGN listeners really did transfer the curse to the Astros when they and their goat were denied entrance to Minute Maid Stadium on Monday night."[26] A 9-7 loss to the Reds in the Cubs' final, regular-season road game dropped the team into a tie with the Astros. The Cubbies still had three home games remaining against the Pirates, while the Astros were about to face the Brewers. Chicago's first game of the three-game series with the Pirates was rained out, but the Astros lost a game to the Brewers and fell a half game behind the Cubs. The next day, Chicago swept a double-header against the Pirates to clinch the Central Division crown. Meanwhile, after the goat incident at Minute Maid Stadium, the Astros went 3-4 to close out the season—finishing the season in second place, one game behind the Chicago Cubs. Whether the curse will take hold in Houston remains to be seen. But for the record, the Houston Astros have won neither a pennant nor a championship since they came into the league in 1962—the team's drought stands at forty-two years.[27]

It was the Cubs' first Central Division title, coming fourteen years after they won their last Eastern Division title and five years after the team made the 1998 playoffs as a wild card team. The team closed out the regular season against the Pirates, retiring former Cub Ron Santo's number 10 jersey in a pregame ceremony, before losing the game 3-2.[28] While the club had lost 95 games the previous year, the team ended the 2003 season with a record of 88-74 and Cubs fans set an attendance record at Wrigley Field (2,962,630).[29]

Chicago headed to Atlanta for the best-of-five-games division series. In the opening game, Kerry Wood struck out twenty batters and earned a 4-2 victory over the Braves. But Atlanta fought back to even the series with a 5-3 win the next day. The teams then traveled to Chicago for the third and fourth games, with the Cubs and Braves even in the best-of-five series. The Cubbies needed to win two more games to reach the National League Championship Series for the first time since 1945. Many Chicago fans now believed that the Curse of the Billy Goat was a "thing of the past and that time and a new attitude have absolved the Cubbies of the hex from Billy Sianis."[30]

From the start of the season, Cubs management and Baker had taken a different tack with the Billy Goat Curse than they had in previous seasons. In February, prior to the season opener, Baker told Jay Mariotti of the *Chicago Sun-Times* the following about the curse: "If you stop talking about it, I think it goes away, and we start winning."[31] Rather than embracing it or trying to publicly end it yet again, they chose to break the curse outright with positive attitude and good play. The Cubs hoped that with a successful season or streak of successful seasons they could forever banish all mention of the goat from the mouths of Chicago Cubs fans. When asked about the curse, they downplayed and ignored it. Instead, they stressed that the Cubs, not history or a curse, controlled the club's destiny. The approach appeared to be working well.

While being interviewed by a local television reporter before game three of the division series against Atlanta, one fan commented: "I think the Billy Goat Curse is beat now. We beat the curse. The curse is over now. We've got it. We've got it. There's no curse anymore."[32] It was audacious talk, considering the Braves had the best regular season record in the National League and were favored to win the pennant, and the series was even after two games. However, "Baker's Boys" had a new and tougher attitude, and the fans were beginning to catch it.[33] For many, the Curse of the Billy Goat was a thing of the past.

Pitching was the key during the third game, and Mark Prior's two-hitter helped beat the Braves 3-1. However, on October 5, 2003, Atlanta beat the Chicago Cubs 6-4 at Wrigley Field to even the series 2-2. The Cubs were not to be deterred though, and the following night Kerry Wood earned his second win of the series with a 5-1 victory over the Braves. The Cubs had finally won their first postseason series since 1908.

Following the division series win over the Braves, many fans were quick to reiterate that the Curse of the Billy Goat had finally been beaten. Believers in the goat hex were suddenly few and far between. Yet, not everyone was ready to declare the Curse of the Billy Goat dead, and believers in the curse still could be found amongst Cubs fans. One person wrote to the *Chicago Tribune* and reminded Chicago that the hex had not yet been beaten: "I hate to burst everyone's bubble, but the Curse of the Chicago Cubs has '*not*' yet been lifted.... Beating Atlanta did not let the Cubs advance to the World Series.... Don't count your pennants until they're flying."[34]

Despite the Cubs' success in winning their first division series against the favored Atlanta Braves and the club's best efforts to downplay the Curse of the Billy Goat throughout the season, the media began to make the goat hex a hot topic throughout the country. Meanwhile, Boston, with its own Curse of the Bambino, had won three straight games over the Oakland Athletics to win the American League Division Series. The prospects of the Chicago Cubs and the Boston Red Sox, with dueling curses, playing against each other in the 2003 World Series was enticing to both fans and television producers. And the media did all it could to help promote both baseball curses. Throughout the National League Championship Series and the American League Championship Series, a curse mania of sorts took over as the national media exploded with talk about the curses. The dream matchup of a "Cubs-Red Sox series would have been one of the most attractive ever," wrote Jay Mariotti of the *Chicago Sun-Times*.[35] Even the *New York Times*, as Jay Mariotti of the *Chicago Sun-Times* noted, was pulling for a "Cubs-Red Sox series," despite the fact that the Yankees were very much alive in the playoffs.[36] "We find it hard to resist the emotional tug and symmetrical possibilities of a series between teams that seem to have been put on Earth to tantalize and then crush their zealous fans." [37]

The only obstacle between the Cubs and their first National League pennant in fifty-eight years was the Florida Marlins, who had upset the favored San Francisco Giants. The Cubs had beaten the Marlins in four of six meetings during the season, and Chicago fans believed that their team was better. Although there was only a marginal difference between the two teams' overall season records, the Cubs were favored to win the series. Nonetheless, one Florida sportswriter predicted that if the billy goat was not seen in Wrigley Field, the Marlins' chances would be much better. "If they don't hear, see or smell Billy Goat and owner Sam Sianis in the ballpark, the odds of the Marlins reaching their second World Series in seven years will most assuredly improve." [38]

On October 7, 2003, the Chicago Cubs played in their third National League Championship Series in nineteen years with Ron Santo's number 10 jersey hanging in the dugout for luck and no billy goat in the ballpark.[39] "Sosa's dramatic two-out, two-run, ninth inning home run sent game 1 into extra innings."[40] But an eleventh-inning home run by Florida's Mike Lowell beat the Cubs 9-8. The Cubs responded the next day with a 12-3 rout of the Marlins before 39,562 fans at Wrigley Field. Two days later, on October 10, 2003, the Cubs went up 2-1 in the series by beating the Marlins in Pro Player Stadium in eleven innings by a score of 5-4. The next evening, the Cubs won their third game of the series, beating the Marlins 8-3. On the brink of winning their first National League pennant in fifty-eight years, the Cubs were shut out by the Florida Marlins in game five. Still, the Cubbies headed back to Chicago with a 3-2 lead in the series.

In preparation for game six of the National League Championship Series, Sam Sianis intended to take "Billy" the goat to Wrigley Field. "If his goat was not invited into the stadium, his goat would be very disappointed," he told a reporter before the game.[41] Although Sianis brought the goat to Wrigley Field before the game, no invitation to enter the stadium was forthcoming, and he and the goat remained outside the main entrance of the ballpark. Still, many Cubs fans seemingly no longer placed much weight on the hex and, with Mark Prior pitching, they were confident that the Cubbies would win the pennant that night. One fan even lugged to the stadium a sign that read "What Curse?" and stood outside the main entrance near Sianis and the goat. Other fans marched into the stadium wearing "Goatbusters" T-shirts announcing that they "ain't afraid of no Goat."[42] As the game progressed, there was little sign of the Curse of the Billy Goat. By the eighth inning Prior was pitching a 3-0 shutout, and victory seemed almost a foregone conclusion to the ecstatic fans who were already starting to celebrate in the streets of Chicago. "Vendors had 2003 National Champions souvenir shirts stashed. Clubhouse officials had bottles of champagne chilling. Snapshots of the 1908 World Series champion Cubs were being shown on T.V."[43]

The eighth inning started out well for the Cubs when the Marlins' Mike Mordecai flied out to left field. However, the next batter, Juan Pierre, hit a double to left. With only five outs needed for the Cubs to make their first World Series appearance in fifty-eight years, Luis Castillo hit a pop-fly foul down the left field line. Moises Alou raced to the railing and was about to catch the foul ball for the second out of the inning, when the ball hit the hand of a fan, Steve Bartman, disrupting Alou's opportunity to make the catch. The Cubs left fielder was visibly upset at the fan, and the crowd was upset as well.[44] "Moments after the incident, fans in the section were booing Bartman and calling for him to be tossed. Several fans chanted in unison, 'Get him out.'"[45] When a fan later offered some support to Bartman by saying that Alou couldn't have caught the ball anyway, someone shouted back, "It cost us the game, pal!"[46]

"Instead of being the second out of the inning, Luis Castillo eventually walked, and the Marlins had men on first and third. It was still 3-0 Cubs, but a shiver ran up and down the spine of Wrigley Field," reported Rick Morrissey of the *Chicago Tribune* the next morning.[47] A single to left field by Ivan "Pudge" Rodriguez scored Pierre, and the Cubs' lead was trimmed to 3-1. Then Alex Gonzalez muffed Miguel Cabrera's bouncer to short and the bases were loaded. When Derrek Lee slammed a double to the outfield, both Castillo and Rodriguez crossed home plate, tying the game 3-3. Baker replaced Mark Prior with Kyle Farnsworth, but the Cubbies' worst nightmare was about to unfold—an intentional walk, a sacrifice fly, another intentional walk, a double to left, and a single to center resulted in five more runs before Luis Castillo's pop-up ended the inning.[48] The Cubs, who were only five outs from their first National League pennant in fifty-eight years, were now down 8-3 in the bottom of the eighth inning. After the disastrous eighth inning, the Cubs were unable to respond with any runs of their own. The Marlins closed out the remaining two innings to even the series at three games apiece. Chicago fans left Wrigley Field stunned and shaken, in disbelief of what transpired. It was only natural that people would begin to claim that the Curse of the Billy Goat had, once again, struck the Cubs. Rick Morrissey summed up many fans' feelings in the *Chicago Tribune* the next day:

> If you're keeping score, it goes: Billy Goat curse, 1969, 1984, 1989 and a swarthy guy with a chisel waiting to etch a new line on the headstone.[49]

Dusty Baker steadfastly denied that it was the curse that caused the fateful eight-run inning. "History has nothing to do with this game," he flatly stated.[50] Reminding the media that there was still one game left to be played and that it would be played in Chicago, Baker commented, "I like our chances."[51] The players also seemed ready to put game six behind them, looking to win game seven and the series the following night. Nonetheless, the media and some Cubs fans had a harder time closing the book on the eight-run, eighth-inning fiasco. Jay Mariotti of the *Chicago Sun-Times* acknowledged that it would be hard for Cubs fans to not think the worst:

> If they lose, face the reality of Cub life. The ballpark is cursed. The franchise is cursed. The entire culture is cursed.[52]

Reporting "the view from Florida," Mike Berardino wrote: "Five outs. That's all the Chicago Cubs needed to end 58 years of the Billy Goat Curse."[53] The words "five outs" will likely ring in the minds of Cubs fans for years to come.

Game seven started out badly for the Cubs after Miguel Cabrera slammed a three-run home run in the first inning. Yet, the Cubs fought back to tie the game in the third. The Cubs added two more runs in the fourth inning to take a 5-3 lead, but they couldn't hold the lead and finally lost the game 9-6. "In losing their third in a row, the Cubs sent a Wrigley Field crowd of 39,574 home to ponder the team's World Series-less famine that has lasted since 1945," noted one writer.[54] Another reporter observed, "The Cubs' elimination—after leading the series 3-1—adds another chapter to their long history of freaky demise occurring just when hopes are highest. The dominant theme of those woeful years has been the so-called 'Curse of the Billy Goat.'"[55]

The 2003 Chicago Cubs, in Dusty Baker's first year as manager, got closer to winning a National League pennant than any other Cubs team since 1945. From the start of the season, the club had a new and positive attitude. Baker had downplayed talk of the Cubbies' history of late-season collapses and the Curse of the Billy Goat. As the season progressed, the team gained a tougher, "no holds barred" attitude. Uncharacteristically, the team finished the month of September winning more games than it lost and, in the process, won the National League Central Division title. The Division Series victory over the Atlanta Braves exorcised the demons from the 1984 collapse to the San Diego Padres—just as the 1984 team had cured the club's "Big Hurt" from the 1969 flop. Nonetheless, for all the success of the 2003 Chicago Cubs, the team will always be remembered for its eight-run, eighth-inning collapse to the Florida Marlins with only five outs to go to win the National League pennant.

Curse theorists maintain that there is little, if any, explanation for the Cubs eighth-inning collapse following the "fan in the stands" incident other than the conclusion that the team is cursed. Yet, as strange as it seems, eight-run, eighth-inning games do occur more frequently than most fans realize. In fact, it happened on at least two other occasions during the 2003 baseball season. Atlanta beat the Mets 11-8, with an eight-run eighth inning on July 20, 2003, and Baltimore accomplished the same feat against Toronto on July 4, 2003.[56] Of course, these earlier games did not have a World Series trip on the line.

In a baseball season that started with the Cubs downplaying the Curse of the Billy Goat and ended with them finishing closer to going to the World Series than any other Cubs team since 1945, there is a strange sense of irony. Once again, the Cubs will have to "wait till next year" to end the club's drought of National League pennants. But talk of the Cubs' history of collapses and the Curse of the Billy Goat will be more deafening in the coming seasons than it ever was before.

10

TRUTH ABOUT BASEBALL CURSES

On October 16, 2003, the night following the Cubs' eighth-inning demise to the Marlins, the Boston Red Sox and the New York Yankees played game seven of the American League Championship Series. In the eighth inning, the Red Sox held a 5-2 lead and were five outs from going to the World Series, but the Yankees scored three runs in the inning and went on to win the American League pennant. As with the Cubs the night before, it was only natural that some Boston fans, as they left Yankee Stadium, would begin to blame the Curse of the Bambino for their team's loss. Only a few days earlier, the country was abuzz with talk about the potential matchup in the World Series of the dueling curses of the Chicago Cubs and the Boston Red Sox.

There are other so-called baseball curses as well—The Curse of Shoeless Joe Jackson (Chicago White Sox -1919),[1] the Curse of Bobby Bragan (Cleveland Indians -1958),[2] the Curse of Rocky Colavito (Cleveland Indians -1960),[3] the lesser-known Fred Merkle Curse (Chicago Cubs - 1908),[4] and a corollary Cubs hex called the Ex-Cub Factor.[5] Although not specific to baseball, the *Sports Illustrated* Cover Curse is often discussed by the media.[6]

The White Sox since 1919 have "appeared in only one World Series and lost."[7] Some people suggest that the misfortunes of the White Sox started after the "Black Sox" scandal of 1919, when eight members of the team, including Shoeless Joe Jackson, were accused of throwing the World Series and were banned from the league forever. Cleveland manager Bobby Bragan was fired during the 1958 season and reportedly went "out to second base the night he was fired and called down a curse upon the team" that they would never win another pennant.[8] Two years later, the Indians traded Rocky Colavito to Detroit and played "hideous baseball for the next 34 years."[9] The Cubs have lost seven straight World Series appearances (1910, 1918, 1929, 1932, 1935, 1938, 1945) and have not won a World Series since 1908, causing some people to suggest that the team suffers from a curse based on what they did to Fred Merkle in 1908—the last year they won a World Series. And some curse theorists believe that the hex that plagues Cubs players doesn't stop when a player leaves the Cubs—teams with ex-Cubs on their rosters rarely win a World Series. The Ex-Cub factor was discovered by writer Ron Berler and later written about by Mike Royko.[10] According to Royko, "Berler theorized that having once been a Cub infects a player with 'Cubness,' a virus that spreads to his teammates with disastrous results."[11] From 1946 to 1989, twelve teams have gone to the World Series with three or more ex-Cubs on the team. Only one of the twelve teams managed to win the World Series. Royko came up with his own "Modified Ex-Cub Factor"—"A team with no ex-Cubs probably has the edge on a team that has even one."[12] The best example of Royko's modified theory was the 1986 World Series between the Mets (no ex-Cubs) and the Red Sox (one ex-Cub). "And that one, Bill Buckner, suffered the anguish of the winning hit squiggling between his legs."[13] Of course, some Red Sox fans blame the Curse of the Bambino for Buckner's misplay during the 1986 World Series. In any event, Royko maintained that the team with more ex-Cubs likely will lose a World Series.[14]

Baseball curses exist outside the United States as well. In Japan, the Hanshin Tigers have reportedly been plagued by the Curse of the Colonel since 1985.[15] This Nipponese hex has its beginnings following the Tigers 1985 Japanese Championship when a happy mob tore loose a statue of Colonel Harlan Sanders of Kentucky Fried Chicken fame and tossed it into the Dotonbori River—the image reminded fans of the bearded Randy Bass who was the star of the 1985 Tigers. Since that time, the Hanshin Tigers have not won the Japanese World Series. Their latest defeat was by the Fukuoka Daiei Hawks in the 2003 Japanese World Series.[16]

As for the *Sports Illustrated* Cover Curse, some believe that appearing on the cover is akin to the kiss of death. One *Sports Illustrated* writer investigated "all of SI's 2,456 covers and found 913 'jinxes'—a demonstrable misfortune or decline in performance following a cover appearance roughly 37.2 percent of the time."[17] In 1984, the Cubs' Leon Durham was featured on the cover of *Sports Illustrated* and had a Buckner-like misplay during the National League Championship Series.[18] In October 2003, with both the Cubs and the Red Sox still very much alive in postseason play, Red Sox pitcher Pedro Martinez and Cubs pitcher Kerry Wood were featured on the cover of *Sports Illustrated.*[19] Both teams would lose critical postseason games pitched by Martinez and Wood a few days later.

Of course, like all hexes, there are believers and there are nonbelievers. About those who believe in sports curses, one sociologist said, "People have to be taking sports enormously seriously to think that there's a cosmic plan to keep them out of the winner's circle."[20] However, a common belief is that if a person believes something bad is going to happen, it will happen. One psychiatrist noted: "Teams thinking they're cursed doesn't help. Our conscious usually complies and we make errors that we feared we'd make. A lot of it is self-fulfilling prophecy."[21]

Superstition in baseball and in other sports has been a part of American society for as long as organized teams have battled on playing fields. Rituals abound, such as wearing "rally caps" at the end of a game in hopes of a come-from-behind victory, wearing the same clothes while on a streak, or performing the same routine each day before a game. With so much underlying belief in superstitions, it's no wonder that some people believe in curses as well. "If you have recurrent patterns and there is no explanation, we'll [people will] rush in to provide one," a psychologist has suggested.[22]

With all the media attention focused on the Cubs and Red Sox during the 2003 postseason, it was only natural that some people would begin to compare the curses to determine which is worse. In fact, one Yankees fan was holding a sign that read "Whose Curse is Worse?" when "Aaron Boone's 11th-inning walkoff home run sent the New York Yankees into the World Series against the Florida Marlins," and thereby sent the Boston Red Sox back to their hotel rooms to start packing their bags for the return trip home.[23]

The Curse of the Bambino is often considered the most famous of the baseball hexes. Although the curse supposedly traces its beginning to Babe Ruth's trade to the New York Yankees in 1919, it's a rather recent hex—not really gathering public attention until after Dan Shaughnessy's book *The Curse of the Bambino* hit the bookshelves in 1990.[24] Today, the Bambino Curse has taken on a life of its own. As Shaughnessy noted:

> In addition to the hardcover, paperback, and audiocassette editions of the original work, the Curse has spawned a screenplay, a rock song, a musical, and a board game. The Curse Web site and CD-ROM can't be far behind. There was even a reference to the Curse on the popular TV quiz show, *Who Wants to Be a Millionaire?*[25]

The Red Sox have played in four World Series (1946, 1967, 1975, 1986) without winning a championship. And the team's last championship goes back to 1918, causing some curse theorists to believe that there is no human explanation for the inability of the Red Sox to win a championship in four tries. Nonetheless, while these losses are particularly troublesome to Red Sox fans, the four World Series defeats do not set Boston's woes apart from the rest of Major League Baseball. Indeed, four other teams in baseball history can match Boston's misfortune—the Brooklyn Dodgers, the Chicago Cubs, the Detroit Tigers, and the New York Giants.[26] Moreover, both the Atlanta Braves and the New York Yankees (a club that has more championships than any other team in baseball history) have had a streak of three appearances in the World Series without winning the championship.[27] And the Major League Baseball record of seven straight World Series appearances without winning a championship, held by the Chicago Cubs and the Brooklyn Dodgers, greatly exceeds the hard luck of the Boston Red Sox.[28] It's simply not that uncommon for baseball teams to appear in the World Series a number of times before winning a championship. The Red Sox championship drought since 1918 may alarm fans, but there's little evidence that the team's misfortunes are due to a curse. Nevertheless, it is somewhat understandable that some fans look elsewhere for explanations for the team's dry spell. Still, both the White Sox (1917) and the Cubs (1908) have gone longer without a championship than the Boston Red Sox (1918).[29] Of course, the fact that other teams have suffered the same disappointments and worse provides little comfort to those Red Sox fans who insist that the Curse of the Bambino is to blame for their setbacks. Indeed, their curse-fever may be heightened by the belief that both Chicago teams are cursed as well.

Although the Curse of the Billy Goat (1945) does not go back as far as the Curse of the Bambino (1919) and lacks its notoriety, it became a part of baseball lore long before the Bambino hex was even named. The Curse of the Billy Goat, once merely a Chicago urban legend, has also taken on a life of its own. There are "Goatbuster" T-shirts, "Cursed" and "Reverse the Curse" buttons, Curse parodies of songs, posters, and other commercial ventures promoted and sold on the Internet. Several movies have been made with the hard-luck Cubs serving as the backdrop for the plot. Another screenplay is in the works that will feature the Cubs' latest 2003 collapse.

In contrast to other so-called "curses," the Curse of the Billy Goat, whether one chooses to believe in curses or not, is based on an actual curse uttered by Billy Goat Sianis in game four of the 1945 World Series. Since that time the Cubbies have come close to winning but still have not won a National League pennant. No other team in baseball history has gone longer without winning a pennant or a World Championship. Yet, other baseball teams have also gone a considerable time without capturing a pennant. The Chicago White Sox have not won a pennant since 1959, only fourteen years fewer than the Cubs.[30] Several teams in baseball have never won a pennant in their club's history—the Houston Astros have not won a pennant since 1962, the Texas Rangers since 1961, and the Montreal Expos since 1969.[31]

A pennant would bring much joy to Cubville and would go a long way in exorcising the demons of the Cubs' past, including the dread Curse of the Billy Goat. Upon that momentous occasion, curse believers will declare that the goat hex has been broken. Nevertheless, it won't take long for curse theorists to rehabilitate the goat's power if the Cubs fail to consistently win pennants. And a pennant without a World Series Championship would be bittersweet to Cubs fans and possibly the ultimate torture—extending to eight the team's streak of World Series appearances without a championship. Of course, curse theorists will claim that the Curse of Fred Merkle was lying in wait since 1945 for the Cubs to, once again, play in the World Series—dashing the team's hopes with another World Series failure.

Still, until the Chicago Cubs win another pennant, many fans will maintain that the Curse of the Billy Goat is alive and well and that it can be found in the friendly confines of Wrigley Field.

EPILOGUE

"The BLEAT GOES ON—'Goat Curse' lives: Cubs' pennant drought reaches 58 years," one *Chicago Tribune* headline read the morning after the Cubs lost game seven of the National League Championship Series.[1] After the bizarre eight-run eighth inning two nights before, it was only natural that people would begin to claim that the Curse of the Billy Goat had, once again, struck the Cubs. And the dominant theme in the media following the Cubs' game seven loss was the Curse of the Billy Goat.

Following the Florida Marlins' victory over the New York Yankees in the 2003 World Series, the discussion of the Curse of the Billy Goat abated somewhat but continued to weigh heavily on the consciousness of Cubs fans and some members of the news media. On December 1, 2003, the infamous "Bartman ball," dubbed "Little Barty" by ESPN hosts, was sold at auction for $113,824.16.[2] There would be no escaping the curse talk throughout the off-season or in the year to come. Indeed, the curse has already received more recognition by the media in 2004 than any other preseason since its inception in 1945. At the January 2004 Chicago Cubs Convention, Dusty Baker was asked about the "biggest surprise in his first year as Cubs manager."[3] Baker responded, "The strength and magnitude of the goat."[4] "I've never seen an animal get this kind of recognition and power."[5] Baker concluded, "We'd like to get rid of that goat."[6] Baker's words echo the comments made by 1994 Cubs manager Tom Trebelhorn ten years earlier, "That goat's got to go. That's all there is to it."[7]

A month after the Cubs Convention, on February 26, 2004, the "Bartman ball" was executed (destroyed) at Harry Caray's

Restaurant in Chicago following a countdown on an MSNBC-televised, live "Predestruction Show," hosted by Keith Olbermann, to rid the Cubs of whatever hex fans attached to it.[8] After the ball was blown to mush, the *Chicago Tribune*'s Deputy Managing Editor Jim Warren told Olbermann his thoughts on what the effect of blowing up the ball might have on the Cubs' curse:

> As far as the curse, I think the folks [after destroying the ball] . . . are living in a dream world. The curse still is with this team, the subsidiary of my company, the Tribune Company, which . . . has developed, traded, or purchased the best pitching staff in the National League. And if they don't get to the World Series this year, the melancholy which can envelop this town, and even turn into depression, remains.[9]

During the off-season, the Cubs added to their roster Greg Maddux, a former Cubs pitcher, who left to join the Atlanta Braves after the 1992 season.[10] His return makes the Cubs' 2004 pitching rotation, which now includes Kerry Wood, Greg Maddux, Mark Prior, Matt Clement, and Carlos Zambrano, one of the best in baseball.[11] With such a good pitching rotation for the 2004 Cubs, the *Chicago Tribune*'s Jim Warren made the following comments about what would happen in Chicago if the Cubs do not win the pennant and who the fans would blame:

> They'll still go back to the Billy Goat . . . . They'll come up with a host of reasons. But, now, given the corporatization of American sports, they're probably going to start blaming me [Warren] and other managers at the Tribune Company. I had nothing to do with this.[12]

Although Jim Warren may not be personally responsible for the Cubs' misfortunes over the years, it is no small irony that the Tribune

Co. now owns the Chicago Cubs (who would like to end the Billy Goat Curse) and that the hex has been kept alive and perpetuated over the past fifty-eight years to a large extent by articles published in the *Chicago Tribune*. Although the Curse of the Billy Goat got its start based on the actions of P. K. Wrigley in 1945, it was during the period the Tribune Co. owned the Cubs that the curse made the transformation from an urban legend to one of the most famous baseball curses of all time.

Tickets for the 2004 Chicago Cubs home games went on sale at the end of February, and fans bought over 572,000 tickets in one day—a major-league ticket sales record.[13] No doubt the ticket sales reflect the high expectations that fans have for the upcoming season. In addition to signing Maddux, the team acquired first baseman Derrek Lee from the Marlins and the majority of the club's veterans are returning for the 2004 campaign, causing many sports prognosticators to pick the Chicago Cubs to win the National League Central Division in 2004. Nevertheless, history is not on the Cubbies' side since they have not had back-to-back postseasons since 1908—the last time they won a World Series.

There's no doubt that many loyal Cubs fans, once the 2004 season begins, will steadfastly maintain that there is no Cubs curse and that the Cubbies will win a National League pennant and a World Series Championship in 2004—the club's first pennant since 1945 and first World Series Championship since 1908. Nevertheless, curse theorists will hold fast to the belief that the curse cannot be beaten and must be lifted in order for the Cubs to win a pennant.

"Acknowledgement of the goat curse could return the Cubs to that quirky part of their support they are trying to distance."[14] However, with such high expectations for the Cubs in 2004, is there any reason for the Cubs not to do whatever it takes to win a pennant and championship? In addition to good, solid play throughout the 2004 season, the following five suggestions (for those that believe in curses and such) might help the Cubs appease the goat curse and the baseball gods (if there are any):

1) Invite Sam Sianis and the goat into Wrigley Field *a la* 1984 since the Cubs historically seem to do better when the goat is invited into the stadium;

2) Fly a Greek flag over Wrigley Plaza or Wrigley Field to appease Billy Goat Sianis' little-known Greek flag Curse;[15]

3) Make September 23rd Fred Merkle Day at Wrigley Field (Merkle was a Chicago Cubs player for four years), thus offering an apology for the incident that occurred in 1908 that helped the Cubs win the pennant that year (their last) and wrongfully tainted Merkle's major league career;

4) When the Cubs play in the postseason, let the goat into the stadium—and let the goat travel to the other teams' field for away games; and

5) Be good to the goat since, as Sam Sianis has noted, "the franchise must respect the goat."[16]

Go Cubbies!

Notes and Sources

Chapter One. ENTER THE GOAT

1. *Chicago Times*, October 6, 1945. A caption to a photograph published in the newspaper showing the waiting crowd read: "Welcome Cubs home—Here is part of the huge crowd that jammed the Union Station last night to welcome victorious Cubs home." One of the cheering fans at Union Station that night was reportedly William "Billy Goat" Sianis who the next day was ejected along with his pet goat from Wrigley Field and in response placed a curse on the Cubs. Condon, David, "Cubs' Hex Lingers On", *Chicago Tribune,* May 23, 1972.

2. The Chicago Cubs' last World Series Championship in 1908 came against the Detroit Tigers.

3. Desmond, Dan, "Cubs' Home Gets Facial," *Chicago Herald-American*, October 3, 1945.

4. Liska, Jerry, *Chicago Times*, October 6, 1945.

5. Rhone, Alan, "He's in! 3-day wait for Series pays off," *Chicago Times*, October 6, 1945. *Times* Staff Correspondent Alan Rhone chronicled his wait in line for tickets since October 3, which earned him the distinction of being the first in line to enter Wrigley Field. Nevertheless, Rhone "gave his place" in line to Art "Happy" Felsch, "the Milwaukee record-holder" who had been first in line for "17 other World Series games."

6. Kupcinet, Irv, "Kup's Column," *Chicago Tribune*, October 9, 1945. The goat's ticket hangs on the wall of the Billy Goat Tavern.

7. Granger, William, "A City Landmark—Billy Goat," *Chicago Tribune*, December 26, 1967.

8. Ibid.

9. Parnell, Sean, "Billy Goat Tavern Review," September 30, 2001, ChicagoBarProject.com.

10. Cromie, Robert, "Billy Goat Sianis Dead at 76," *Chicago*

Tribune, October 23, 1970. A copy of the letter to the State Department can be found on the wall of the original Billy Goat Tavern.

11. Granger, William, "A City Landmark—Billy Goat," *Chicago Tribune*, December 26, 1967.

12. *Chicago Times*, October 6, 1945. The evening newspaper managed to photograph the incident and published the photograph that night. The caption to the photograph read: "Getting whose goat?—Squad of ushers at Wrigley field find combined efforts fail to keep Billy Sianis and his pet billy goat out of the ball park for today's World Series game between Detroit Tigers and Chicago Cubs." The animal wore a sign that read, "We Got Detroit's Goat."

13. Kessler, Gene, "World Series Sidelights," *Chicago Times*, October 7, 1945. Woodard, Milt, "Trout Puts on His Spectacles Again But the Cubs Really Needed Them," *Chicago Sun*, October 7, 1945. According to Woodard, "Andy Frain employed a dozen walkie-talkies in directing his 500 employees—200 usherettes and 300 ushers—about the park."

14. Kessler, Gene, "This goat had a seat," *Chicago Times*, October 7, 1945.

15. Ibid.

16. Cannon, Ralph, "Prim's Best Just Not Good Enough," *Chicago Herald-American*, October 7, 1945.

17. Ward, Arch, "In the Wake of the News," *Chicago Tribune*, October 7, 1945. Andrew T. "Andy" Frain owned Andy Frain Services which ran the ushers, dressed in blue and gold uniforms, at Wrigley Field.

18. St. Clair, Stacy, "Fans not speaking curse word," *Daily Herald*, October 13, 2003.

19. McAteer, Jim "Cubs battling the Billy Goat curse," WNDU NewsCenter 16, on-line edition, October 15, 2003.

20. Cromie, Robert, "Billy Goat Sianis Dead at 76," *Chicago Tribune*, October 23, 1970.

21. Royko, Mike, "Let's All Drink To Billy Goat," *Chicago Tribune*, October 23, 1970.

22. Stern, Jan and Michael, "Live From Chicago . . . It's the Billy Goat Tavern," *Gourmet*, September 2003.

23. Ibid.

24. Ibid. Billy Goat Sianis and Bill Charuchas, another Greek

immigrant, pioneered the habit of the counterman yelling out to customers. Today, the same custom is maintained at the original Billy Goat Tavern.

25. Sullivan, Paul, "Foiled again . . . and again—Curse talk still getting Cubs' goat," *Chicago Tribune*, May 6, 1997.

Chapter Two. TINKER TO EVERS TO CHANCE

1. The Chicago White Sox (second longest drought) have not won a World Series since 1917 and the Boston Red Sox (third longest drought) have not won a World Series since 1918. Baseball-Reference.com.

2. MLB.com, Chicago Cubs History.

3. Ibid.

4. Ibid.

5. Ibid.

6. Ibid. Pierce, Franklin, "A Sad Lexicon," *New York Evening Mail*, July 10, 1910. The word gonfalon refers to a flag or pennant.

7. Chicago Cubs History, MLB.com.

8. Shaughnessy, Dan, *The Curse Of The Bambino* (New York: Penguin Books, 2000).

9. Ibid., p. 31. According to Shaughnessy, "The sales contract was signed on Friday, December 26, 1919."

10. Baseball-Reference.com.

11. Deford, Frank, "Curses, From Boston to Chicago to Japan, baseball teams can't shake bad luck," SportsIllustrated.com, September 24, 2003.

12. Dryden, Charles, "Game Ends In Tie May Go To Cubs," *Chicago Tribune*, September 24, 1908.

13. Ibid.

14. Ibid.

15. Ibid.

16. Ibid.

17. Deford, Frank, "Curses, From Boston to Chicago to Japan, baseball teams can't shake bad luck," SportsIllustrated.com, September 24, 2003.

18. Burnell, Tim, "I Call My Cane 'Merkle,'" www.NetShrine.com, not dated.

19. Anderson, David W., *More Than Merkle: A History of the Best and Most Exciting Baseball Season in Human History* (Lincoln:

University of Nebraska Press, 2000). Forward by Keith Olbermann; Baseball-Almanac.com.

Chapter Three. THE CURSE YEARS

1. Baseball-Reference.com.
2. Ibid.
3. Granger, William, "A City Landmark—Billy Goat," *Chicago Tribune*, December 26, 1967.
4. Castle, George, *The Million-to-One-Team: Why the CHICAGO CUBS Haven't Won a Pennant Since 1945* (South Bend: Diamond Communications, Inc., 2000), p. 15.
5. Newman, Mark, "Chicago holding its breath for Cubs," October 14, 2003.
6. Condon, David, "In the Wake of the News," *Chicago Tribune*, April 15, 1969.
7. Ibid.
8. Castle, George, *The Million-to-One-Team: Why the CHICAGO CUBS Haven't Won a Pennant Since 1945* (South Bend: Diamond Communications, Inc., 2000), p. 73.
9. Ibid.
10. Ibid.
11. Baseball-Reference.com.
12. Ibid.
13. Granger, William, "A City Landmark—Billy Goat," *Chicago Tribune*, December 26, 1967.
14. Ibid. Billy Goat Sianis officially lifted the curse in April 1969. Nineteen years earlier, in September 1950, P. K. Wrigley sent a letter to Sianis apologizing for the goat incident and asked that the hex be lifted. According to David Condon, Sianis refused to end the hex at that time. However, William Granger reported two years earlier, in 1967, that Sianis had accepted Wrigley's apology and lifted the curse. Condon, David, "In the Wake of the News," *Chicago Tribune*, April 15, 1969; Newman, Mark, "Comparing the curses," MLB.com, October 17, 2003.
15. Royko, Mike, "It was Wrigley, not some goat, who cursed Cubs," *Chicago Tribune*, March 21, 1997.

Chapter Four. THE BIG HURT

1. *Chicago Tribune,* April 6, 1969.
2. *Chicago Tribune,* April 1, 1969.
3. *Chicago Tribune,* April 8, 1969.
4. *Chicago Tribune,* April 9, 1969.
5. Ibid.
6. Condon, David, "In the Wake of the News," *Chicago Tribune,* April 15, 1969.
7. *Chicago Tribune,* April 21, 1969.
8. *Chicago Tribune,* May 16, 1969.
9. *Chicago Tribune,* May 17, 1969.
10. Condon, David, *Chicago Tribune,* June 3, 1969.
11. Ibid.
12. *Chicago Tribune,* June 6, 1969.
13. Gill, Donna, "Strange Things Happening," *Chicago Tribune,* June 7, 1969.
14. Ibid.
15. *Chicago Tribune,* June 23, 1969.
16. Ibid.
17. Ibid.
18. *Chicago Tribune,* June 10, 1969.
19. Ibid.
20. *Chicago Tribune,* June 20, 1969.
21. Ibid.
22. *Chicago Tribune,* July 1, 1969.
23. Ibid.
24. *Chicago Tribune,* July 8, 1969.
25. *Chicago Tribune,* July 26, 1969.
26. *Chicago Tribune,* July 11, 1969. The Cubs players received letters from mothers complaining that the players were not signing autographs for their children.
27. Ibid.
28. "Leo to Explain at Meeting Today With Wrigley," *Chicago Tribune,* July 29, 1969.
29. Markus, Robert, "Leo is being Leo—So Why change him?," *Chicago Tribune,* July 30, 1969.
30. Ibid.

31. *Chicago Tribune,* August 16, 1969.
32. Prell, Edward, *Chicago Tribune,* September 8, 1969.
33. Ibid.
34. *Chicago Tribune,* September 9, 1969.
35. *Chicago Tribune,* September 11, 1969.
36. Claerbaut, David, *Durocher's Cubs: The Greatest Team That Didn't Win* (Taylor Publishing, 2000), p. 6.
37. "The Big Hurt—Reflections from the '69 Cubs and Mets on the dramatic season that won't go away," *Chicago Tribune,* August 27, 1989.
38. Ibid.
39. Ibid.
40. Condon, David, "In the Wake of the News," *Chicago Tribune,* September 29, 1969.
41. Ibid.
42. Attiyeh, Mike, *Who Was Traded For Lefty Grove? Baseball's Fun Facts And Serious Trivia* (Baltimore: Johns Hopkins University Press, 2002), p. 130.
43. Ibid., p. 131.
44. Ibid.
45. Ibid.

Chapter Five. WAIT TILL NEXT YEAR

1. *Chicago Tribune,* April 10, 1970.
2. Ibid.
3. *Chicago Tribune,* April 9, 1970.
4. *Chicago Tribune,* April 15, 1970.
5. Condon, David, "Cubs' Hex Lingers On," *Chicago Tribune,* May 23, 1972.
6. Condon, David, "In the Wake of the News," *Chicago Tribune,* April 15, 1969.
7. Markus, Robert, *Chicago Tribune,* June 15, 1973.
8. Markus, Robert, *Chicago Tribune,* June 17, 1973.
9. Letter to sports editor, *Chicago Tribune,* June 15, 1973.
10. The Chicago White Sox won the 1959 American League pennant but lost to the Los Angeles Dodgers in the World Series.
11. *Chicago Tribune,* June 20, 1973. Since 1959, the White Sox

have won four division titles; however, they have not won another pennant.

12. Logan, Bob, *Chicago Tribune,* June 28, 1973.

13. Ibid.

14. Condon, David, "If Cubs blow it, look for goat," *Chicago Tribune*, July 6, 1973. Billy Goat Sianis once pledged "the Cubs never will win a pennant as long as I'm alive . . . . I'm leaving it in my will . . . to my heirs, and to the heirs of my goat, the hex on the Cubs." Whether Sianis made the statement before or after he lifted the hex in April 1969 is not known.

15. Ibid.

16. Ibid.

17. Ibid.

18. Ibid.

19. Ibid.

20. Ibid.

21. Ibid.

22. Ibid. Before the Cubs' collapse in 1973, David Condon teased the Cubs in the *Chicago Tribune* by announcing that Sam Sianis' pet goat Socrates stayed at Oakland Athletics owner Charlie O. Finley's La Porte, Indiana, farm and that if the Athletics and the Cubs made it to the World Series, Finley would allow Sianis and his goat to attend the games in Oakland's official box. Condon, David, "A Finley-Wrigley series?," *Chicago Tribune,* July 7, 1973.

23. Israel, David, "New Cub Hex?—Billy Goat XII suffers same indignity as forebear in 1945," *Chicago Daily News*, July 5, 1973.

24. *Chicago Tribune,* May 29, 1973.

25. *Chicago Tribune,* August 7, 1973.

26. *Chicago Tribune,* June 17, 1981.

27. Ibid.

28. Ibid.

29. Ibid.

30. Ibid.

31. Ibid.

Chapter Six. THE MIRACLE SEASON

1. Jim Frey managed the Kansas City Royals in 1980 and 1981,

winning an American League pennant in 1980.
  2. James, Bill, *Chicago Tribune,* April 1, 1984.
  3. *Chicago Tribune,* April 4, 1984.
  4. *Chicago Tribune,* April 5, 1984.
  5. *Chicago Tribune,* April 8, 1984.
  6. Daley, Steve, *Chicago Tribune,* April 14, 1984.
  7. Ibid.
  8. Ibid.
  9. *Chicago Sun-Times,* April 14, 1984.
  10. *Chicago Tribune,* April 14, 1984.
  11. Lincicome, Bernie, *Chicago Tribune,* April 20, 1984.
  12. *Chicago Tribune,* April 26, 1984.
  13. *Chicago Tribune,* April 27, 1984.
  14. Ibid.
  15. Ibid.
  16. *Chicago Tribune,* April 30, 1984.
  17. *Chicago Tribune,* May 17, 1984.
  18. Ibid.
  19. Holtzman, Jerome, *Chicago Tribune,* May 24, 1984.
  20. *Chicago Tribune,* May 24, 1984.
  21. Verdi, Bob, *Chicago Tribune,* June 4, 1984.
  22. *Sports Illustrated,* June 11, 1984.
  23. *Chicago Tribune,* August 3, 1984.
  24. *Chicago Tribune,* August 9, 1984.
  25. *Chicago Tribune,* September 10, 1984.
  26. *Chicago Tribune,* September 11, 1984.
  27. Daley, Steve, *Chicago Tribune,* September 13, 1984.
  28. *Chicago Tribune,* September 25, 1984.
  29. Mitchell, Fred, *Chicago Tribune,* September 25, 1984.
  30. Ibid.
  31. Ibid.
  32. *Chicago Tribune,* September 27, 1984. The Cubs' 45-36 road record was its best since 1945, and the home record of 51-29 was the best since 1936.
  33. Merkin, Scott, "Hex off, but respect for goat would help title bid," MLB.Com, October 13, 2003; Doshi, Supriya, "Curse still overshadows Cubs," *Daily Illini,* October 17, 2003.
  34. *Chicago Tribune,* October 8, 1984.

35. Doshi, Supriya, "Curse still overshadows Cubs," *Daily Illini*, October 17, 2003.

36. Baseball-Reference.com. The Chicago Cubs' overall record was 96-65 (.596); the San Diego Padres' season record was 92-70 (.568).

37. Ibid.

38. Ibid. The Cubs' National League-leading home record was 51-29 (.638) and the Padres' home record of 48-33 (593) was second best (a tie with the Mets) in the National League.

39. Ibid.

Chapter Seven. THE BOYS OF ZIMMER

1. Baseball-Reference.com.

2. *Chicago Tribune*, August 9, 1988.

3. *Chicago Tribune*, April 5, 1989.

4. Merkin, Scott, "'Billy Goat Curse' officially lifted," MLB.com, October 13, 2003.

5. Margolis, Jon, "Will Chicago lose something if Cubs win?" *Chicago Tribune*, October 5, 1989. The hit play "Bleacher Bums" played to filled seats at the Organic Theatre from June 1989 through the Cubs' postseason games with the Giants.

6. Koppett, Leonard, "'Bonehead' Merkle's retribution could be at hand," *Chicago Tribune*, October 3, 1989.

7. Margolis, Jon, "Will Chicago lose something if Cubs win?" *Chicago Tribune*, October 5, 1989.

8. Lincicome, Bernie, "Day to forget, season to remember," *Chicago Tribune*, October 11, 1989.

9. Royko, Mike, "Let's lay blame where it's due," *Chicago Tribune*, October 11, 1989.

Chapter Eight. LIFTING THE CURSE

1. Baseball-Reference.com, Chicago Cubs History.

2. Tom Trebelhorn managed the Milwaukee Brewers from 1986 to 1991 before becoming manager of the Chicago Cubs in 1994.

3. Baseball-Reference.com, Chicago Cubs History.

4. Lincicome, Bernie, *Chicago Tribune*, May 6, 1997.

5. Ibid.

6. Reaves, Joseph A., "Cubs' streak starting to get manager's goat," *Chicago Tribune*, April 30, 1994.

7. Ibid.

8. Ginnetti, Toni, "Cubs Skipper Might Have More Chats With Fans," *Chicago Sun-Times*, May 1, 1994.

9. Ginnetti, Toni, "Nothing a Goat Couldn't Correct," *Chicago Sun-Times*, May 5, 1994. According to Ginnetti, "Tavern owner Sam Sianis went along with a radio stunt and arrived Wednesday with a stand-in goat—draped in a Cubs jersey and accompanied by 48 pre-ministry students from Waterton, Wis., who own him—to again lift the curse placed on the Cubs by Sianis' father [uncle] when his mascot goat was refused entry to the 1945 World Series."

10. *Chicago Tribune*, May 5, 1994.

11. Ibid.

12. Ginnetti, Toni, "Nothing a Goat Couldn't Correct," *Chicago Sun-Times*, May 5, 1994.

13. *Chicago Tribune*, May 5, 1994.

14. Ibid.

15. Ibid.

16. Ibid.

17. Wojciechowski, Gene, "Trachsel's goal: Shed goat horns," *Chicago Tribune*, February 19, 1996.

18. Ibid.

19. Ginnetti, Toni, "Nothing a Goat Couldn't Correct," *Chicago Sun-Times*, May 5, 1994.

20. Ibid.

21. Wojciechowski, Gene, "Trachsel's goal: Shed goat horns," *Chicago Tribune*, February 19, 1996.

22. Sullivan, Paul, *Chicago Tribune*, March 30, 1997.

23. *Chicago Tribune*, March 19, 1997.

24. Ibid.

25. Royko, Mike, *"It was Wrigley, not some goat, who cursed Cubs," Chicago Tribune*, March 21, 1997.

26. Ibid.

27. Ibid.

28. *Chicago Tribune*, April 5, 1997.

29. Ibid.
30. *Chicago Tribune*, April 8, 1997.
31. Ibid.
32. Sullivan, Paul, "Foiled again . . . and again—Curse talk still getting Cubs' goat," *Chicago Tribune*, May 6, 1997.
33. Mitchell, Fred, *Chicago Tribune*, April 10, 1997.
34. Sullivan, Paul, "Too Soon For A June Swoon?," *Chicago Tribune*, April 11, 1997.
35. Ibid.
36. Sullivan, Paul, "Veteran Cubs call player-only meeting in effort to stop slide," *Chicago Tribune*, April 11, 1997.
37. *Chicago Tribune*, April 16, 1997.
38. *Chicago Tribune*, April 16, 1997.
39. Mitchell, Fred, "Deserves a break today," *Chicago Tribune*, April 17, 1997.
40. Sullivan, Paul, "Cubs' MacPhail preaches patience," *Chicago Tribune*, April 18, 1997.
41. Ibid.
42. Ibid.
43. Knowles, Joe, "Good Morning, Billy Goat," *Chicago Tribune*, April 19, 1997.
44. *Chicago Tribune*, April 20, 1997.
45. *Chicago Tribune*, April 21, 1997.
46. Ibid.
47. Sullivan, Paul, "Foiled again . . . and again—Curse talk still getting Cubs' goat," *Chicago Tribune*, May 6, 1997.
48. Ibid.
49. Ibid.

Chapter Nine. YEAR OF THE GOAT

1. *Chicago Tribune*, November 16, 2002.
2. *Chicago Tribune*, November 20, 2002.
3. Mullin, John, "Baker lets fans know he gets the history," ChicagoSports.com, October 8, 2003.
4. Paul, Noel C., "Can Dusty help Cubs find their mojo?," *Christian Science Monitor*, June 17, 2003.
5. *Chicago Tribune*, April 1, 2003.

6. Morrissey, Rick, *Chicago Tribune*, April 1, 2003.
7. *Chicago Tribune*, June 4, 2003.
8. *Chicago Tribune*, June 12, 2003.
9. *Chicago Tribune (Red Eye)*, June 18, 2003.
10. Ibid.
11. Morrissey, Rick, "Baker raises heat in unusual way," *Chicago Tribune*, July 6, 2003.
12. Ibid.
13. *Chicago Tribune*, July 8, 2003.
14. Sullivan, Paul, *Chicago Tribune*, July 8, 2003.
15. *Chicago Tribune*, July 8, 2003.
16. *Chicago Tribune*, July 11, 2003.
17. *Chicago Tribune*, July 12, 2003.
18. *Chicago Tribune*, September 30, 2003.
19. Morrissey, Rick, "Oh, great, Cubs into magic dust," *Chicago Tribune*, September 5, 2003.
20. Ibid.
21. *Chicago Tribune*, September 6, 2003; September 7, 2003.
22. Sullivan, Paul, *Chicago Tribune*, September 23, 2003.
23. WGN.com
24. Ibid.
25. *Chicago Tribune*, September 25, 2003.
26. Rogers, Phil, *Chicago Tribune*, September 24, 2003.
27. Baseball-Reference.com, Houston Astros History.
28. *Chicago Tribune*, September 29, 2003.
29. Ibid.
30. Yu, Linda, "Has the 'Billy Goat Curse' on the Cubs been lifted?," ABC7Chicago.com, October 3, 2003.
31. Paul, Noel C., "Can Dusty help Cubs find their mojo?," *Christian Science Monitor*, June 17, 2003.
32. Yu, Linda, "Has the 'Billy Goat Curse' on the Cubs been lifted?," ABC7Chicago.com, October 3, 2003.
33. Cubs fans with signs that read "I Believe" could be found in the bleachers for the postseason games.
34. *Chicago Tribune*, "Reader Views," October 11, 2003.
35. Mariotti, Jay, "Cubs love becomes national pastime," *Chicago-Sun-Times*, October 10, 2003.
36. Ibid.

37. Ibid.

38. Fialkov, Harvey, "If Goat shows, Marlins might get wriggly," *Chicago Tribune*, October 7, 2003.

39. *Chicago Tribune*, October 8, 2003.

40. Ibid.

41. Doshi, Supriya, "Curse still overshadows Cubs," *Daily Illini*, October 17, 2003.

42. Ibid.

43. Downey, Mike, "No magic on 8th ball," *Chicago Tribune*, October 15, 2003.

44. *Chicago Tribune*, October 15, 2003.

45. Malcolm, Chris, "Touching off a storm," *Chicago Tribune*, October 15, 2003.

46. Ibid.

47. Morrissey, Rick, "8th inning disaster so Cubs," *Chicago Tribune*, October 15, 2003.

48. *Chicago Tribune*, October 15, 2003.

49. Morrissey, Rick, "8th inning disaster so Cubs," *Chicago Tribune*, October 15, 2003.

50. Ibid.

51. Downey, Mike, "No magic on 8th ball," *Chicago Tribune*, October 15, 2003.

52. Mariotti, Jay, "This is no reach: Cubs curse lives," *Chicago Sun-Times*, October 15, 2003.

53. Berardino, Mike, "Curse kicks in, right on cue," *Chicago Tribune*, October 15, 2003.

54. Weir, Tom, "What the 'hex' is going on," USAToday.com, October 16, 2003.

55. Ibid.

56. "Braves score 8 in eighth inning to down Mets," *Post and Courier* (Charleston.net), July 21, 2003; Toronto v. Baltimore, "How they scored," USAToday.com, July 4, 2003.

Chapter Ten. TRUTH ABOUT BASEBALL CURSES

1. Sullivan, Paul, "Foiled again . . . and again—Curse talk still getting Cubs' goat," *Chicago Tribune*, May 6, 1997.

2. "Witch way to foil curse?," *Chicago Sun-Times,* April 16, 1994.

3. Sullivan, Paul, "Foiled again . . . and again—Curse talk still getting Cubs' goat," *Chicago Tribune*, May 6, 1997.

4. Deford, Frank, "Curses, From Boston to Chicago to Japan, baseball teams can't shake bad luck," SportsIllustrated.com, September 24, 2003.

5. Royko, Mike, "Ex-Cub Factor comes into play," *Chicago Tribune*, October 4, 1989.

6. Wolff, Alexander, "Unraveling the Jinx," SportsIllustrated.com, January 15, 2004.

7. Sullivan, Paul, "Foiled again . . . and again—Curse talk still getting Cubs' goat," *Chicago Tribune*, May 6, 1997.

8. "Witch way to foil curse?" *Chicago Sun-Times*, April 16, 1994.

9. Sullivan, Paul, "Foiled again . . . and again—Curse talk still getting Cubs' goat," *Chicago Tribune*, May 6, 1997.

10. Royko, Mike, "Ex-Cub Factor comes into play," *Chicago Tribune*, October 4, 1989.

11. Ibid.
12. Ibid.
13. Ibid.
14. Ibid.

15. Deford, Frank, "Curses, From Boston to Chicago to Japan, baseball teams can't shake bad luck," SportsIllustrated.com, September 24, 2003.

16. Sloan, Dan, "Hawks Win Japan Series As 'Curse' Bedevils Hanshin," Reuters, October 27, 2003. The Hanshin Tigers lost game seven to the Fukuoka Daiei Hawks, "keeping alive talk of a 'Kentucky Fried curse.'"

17. Wolff, Alexander, "Unraveling the Jinx," SportsIllustrated.com, January 15, 2004.

18. *Sports Illustrated*, June 11, 1984.

19. *Sports Illustrated*, October 13, 2003.

20. Katz, Abram, "The curse: Cubs, Sox beat the odds," MiddletownPress.com," October 17, 2003. Quote attributed to Chris Doob, sociologist at Southern Connecticut State University.

21. Ibid. Quote attributed to Dr. Sidney Ruben, director of the emergency psychiatric services at the Hospital of St. Raphael.

22. Emerson, Bo, "Curses! True or not, they can get our goats in end," *Atlanta Journal-Constitution*, October 17, 2003.

23. Newman, Mark, "Comparing the curses," MLB.Com, October 17, 2003.

24. Shaughnessy, Dan, *The Curse of the Bambino* (New York: E. P. Dutton, 1990).

25. Shaughnessy, Dan, *The Curse of the Bambino* (New York: Penguin Books, 2000), p. 219.

26. Baseball-Reference.com.

27. Ibid.

28. Ibid.

29. Ibid.

30. Sullivan, Paul, "Foiled again . . . and again—Curse talk still getting Cubs' goat," *Chicago Tribune*, May 6, 1997.

31. Baseball-Reference.Com.

EPILOGUE

1. *Chicago Tribune,* October 16, 2004.

2. Leptich, John, "Foul ball touched by Chicago fan to be destroyed at Harry Caray's," *East Valley Tribune* (Mesa, Arizona), February 21, 2004.

3. Sullivan, Paul, "Talk about curse gets Baker's goat, Maddux also tops convention topics," ChicagoSports.com, January 18, 2004.

4. Ibid.

5. Ibid.

6. Ibid.

7. Reaves, Joseph A., "Cubs' streak starting to get manager's goat," *Chicago Tribune*, April 30, 1994.

8. MSNBC "Predestruction Show," hosted by Keith Olbermann on February 26, 2004.

9. Ibid.

10. Armour, Nancy, "Greg Maddux returns to his baseball roots, signs with Chicago Cubs," *Yahoo! Sports Canada*, February 18, 2004.

11. Sullivan, Paul, "Wood named to start opener," ChicagoSports.com, February 28, 2004; Morrissey, Rick, "Curse cure-all drives mission for Maddux," ChicagoSports.com, January 18, 2004.

12. MSNBC "Predestruction Show," hosted by Keith Olbermann on February 26, 2004.

13. Sullivan, Paul, "advanced ticket sales called 'mindboggling,'"

ChicagoSports.com, March 1, 2004.

14. Merkin, Scott, "Hex off, but respect for goat would help title bid," MLB.Com, October 13, 2003.

15. Condon, David, "In the Wake of the News," *Chicago Tribune*, April 15, 1969.

16. Merkin, Scott, "Hex off, but respect for goat would help title bid," MLB.com, October 13, 2003.

BIBLIOGRAPHY

BOOKS

Anderson, David W. *More Than Merkle: A History of the Best and Most Exciting Baseball Season in Human History.* Lincoln: University of Nebraska Press, 2000.

Attiyeh, Mike. *Who Was Traded For Lefty Grove? Baseball's Fun Facts And Serious Trivia.* Baltimore: Johns Hopkins University Press, 2002.

Castle, George. *The Million-to-One-Team: Why the CHICAGO CUBS Haven't Won a Pennant Since 1945.* South Bend: Diamond Communications, Inc., 2000.

Claerbaut, David. *Durocher's Cubs: The Greatest Team That Didn't Win.* Taylor Publishing, 2000.

Shaughnessy, Dan. *The Curse of the Bambino.* New York: Penguin Books, 2000.

ARTICLES

Armour, Nancy, "Greg Maddux returns to his baseball roots, signs with Cubs," *Yahoo! Sports Canada*, February 18, 2004.

Berardino, Mike, "Curse kicks in, right on cue," *Chicago Tribune*, October 15, 2003.

Burnell, Tim, "I call My Cane 'Merkle,'" not dated, NetShrine.com.

Cannon, Ralph, "Prim's Best Just Not Good Enough," *Chicago Herald-American*, October 7, 1945.

Clark, Peter and Sullivan, Tim, "Float like a goat toward obscurity," *San Diego Union-Tribune*, October 16, 2003.

Condon, David, "In the Wake of the News," *Chicago Tribune*, April 15, 1969.

———. "In the Wake of the News," *Chicago Tribune,* September

29, 1969.

———. "Cubs' Hex Lingers On," *Chicago Tribune,* May 23, 1970.

———. "If Cubs blow it, look for goat," *Chicago Tribune*, July 6, 1973.

———. "A Finley-Wrigley series?," *Chicago Tribune*, July 7, 1973.

Couch, Greg, "Crying uncle: Baseball gods get our goat again," Sun-Times.com, October 16, 2003.

Cromie, Robert, "Billy Goat Sianis Dead at 76," *Chicago Tribune*, October 23, 1970.

Deford, Frank, "Curses, From Boston to Chicago to Japan, baseball teams can't shake bad luck," SportsIllustrated.com, September 24, 2003.

Desmond, Dan, "Cubs' Home Gets Facial," *Chicago Herald-American*, October 3, 1945.

Doshi, Supriya, "Curse still overshadows Cubs," *Daily Illini*, October 17, 2003.

Downey, Mike, "No magic on 8th ball," *Chicago Tribune,* October 15, 2003.

Dryden, Charles, "Game Ends In Tie May Go To Cubs," *Chicago Tribune*, September 24, 1908.

Emerson, Bo, "Curses! True or not, they can get our goats in end," *Atlantic Journal-Constitution*, October 17, 2003.

Ettkin, Brian, "In sports, superstition of the way," TimesUnion.com, October 18, 2003.

Fialkov, Harvey, "If Goat shows, Marlins might get wriggly," *Chicago Tribune*, October 7, 2003.

Gill, Donna, "Strange Things Happening," *Chicago Tribune,* June 7, 1969.

Ginnetti, Toni, "Cubs Skipper Might Have More Chats With Fans," *Chicago Sun-Times*, May 1, 1994.

———. "Nothing a Goat Couldn't Correct," *Chicago Sun-Times*, May 5, 1994.

Granger, William, "A City Landmark—Billy Goat," *Chicago Tribune*, December 26, 1967.

Israel, David, "New Cub Hex?—Billy Goat XII suffers same indignity as forebear in 1945," *Chicago Daily News*, July 5, 1973.

Jervis, Rick, "Will Chicago ever give up the goat?," *Chicago Tribune,* January 23, 2004.

Bibliography

Katz, Abram, The curse: Cubs, Sox beat the odds," MiddletownPress.com, October 17, 2003.

Kessler, Gene, "This goat had a seat," *Chicago Times*, October 7, 1945.

Knowles, Joe, "Good Morning, Billy Goat," *Chicago Tribune*, April 19, 1997.

Koppett, Leonard, "'Bonehead' Merkle's retribution could be at hand," *Chicago Tribune*, October 3, 1989.

———. "This goat had a seat," *Chicago Times*, October 7, 1945.

Kupcinet, Irv, "Kup's Column," *Chicago Tribune*, October 9, 1945.

Leptich, John, "Foul ball touched by Chicago fan to be destroyed at Harry Caray's," MercuryNews.com, February 21, 2004.

Liska, Jerry, "Series tickets demand grows," *Chicago Times*, October 6, 1945.

Malcolm, Chris, "Touching off a storm," *Chicago Tribune*, October 15, 2003.

Margolis, Jon, "Will Chicago lose something if Cubs win?" *Chicago Tribune*, October 5, 1989.

Markus, Robert, "Leo is being Leo—So Why change him?," *Chicago Tribune,* July 30, 1969.

Mariotti, Jay, "Cubs love becomes national pastime," *Chicago-Sun-Times*, October 10, 2003.

———. "This is no reach: Cubs curse lives," *Chicago-Sun-Times*, October 15, 2003.

McAteer, Jim, "Cubs battling the Billy Goat curse," WNDU NewsCenter 16, on-line edition, October 15, 2003.

Merkin, Scott, "Hex off, but respect for goat would help title bid," MLB.com, October 13, 2003.

Morrissey, Rick, "Baker raises heat in unusual way," *Chicago Tribune,* July 6, 2003.

———. "Oh, great, Cubs into magic dust," *Chicago Tribune,* September 5, 2003.

———. "Eighth inning disaster so Cubs," *Chicago Tribune,* October 15, 2003.

———. "Curse cure-all drives mission for Maddux," *Chicago Tribune*, January 18, 2004.

Mullin, John, "Baker lets fans know he gets the history," ChicagoSports.com, October 8, 2003.

Muskat, Carrie, "Cubs trip trying to wrap up NLDS," October 4, 2003.

Newman, Mark, "Chicago holding its breath for Cubs," MLB.Com, October 14, 2003.

———. "Comparing the curses," MLB.Com, October 17, 2003.

Parnell, Sean, "Billy Goat Tavern Review," September 30, 2001, ChicagoBarProject.com.

Paul, Noel C., "Can Dusty help Cubs find their mojo?" *Christian Science Monitor*, June 17, 2003.

Pierce, Franklin, "A Sad Lexicon," *New York Evening Mail*, July 10, 1910.

Quinn, T. J., "Curse gets Cubs' goat once more," NYDailyNews.com, October 16, 2003.

Reaves, Joseph A., "Cubs' streak starting to get manager's goat," *Chicago Tribune*, April 30, 1994.

Rhone, Alan, "He's in! 3-day wait for Series pays off," *Chicago Times*, October 6, 1945.

Royko, Mike, "Let's All Drink To Billy Goat," *Chicago Tribune*, October 23, 1970.

———. "Ex-Cub Factor comes into play," *Chicago Tribune*, October 4, 1989.

———. "Let's lay blame where it's due," *Chicago Tribune*, October 11, 1989.

———. "It was Wrigley, not some goat, who cursed Cubs," *Chicago Tribune*, March 21, 1997.

St. Clair, Stacy, "Fans not speaking curse word," *Daily Herald*, October 13, 2003.

Sloan, Dan, "Hawks Win Japan Series As 'Curse' Bedevils Hanshin," *Reuters*, October 27, 2003.

Stern, Jan and Michael, "Live From Chicago . . . It's the Billy Goat Tavern," *Gourmet*, September 2003.

Sternig, Amy, "Can this goat be a curse buster?," MLB.Com, October 15, 2003.

———. "Curses! Does the hex exist?," MLB.Com, October 16, 2003.

Sullivan, Paul, "Veteran Cubs call player-only meeting in effort to stop slide," *Chicago Tribune*, April 11, 1997.

———. "Too Soon For A June Swoon?," *Chicago Tribune*, April 11, 1997.
———. "MacPhail preaches patience," *Chicago Tribune*, April 18, 1997.
———. "Foiled again... and again—Curse talk still getting Cubs' goat," *Chicago Tribune*, May 6, 1997.
———. "Talk about curse gets Baker's goat, Maddux also tops convention topics," ChicagoSports.com, January 18, 2004.
———. "Cubs start running a fever," ChicagoSports.com, February 19, 2004.
———. "Wood named to start opener," ChicagoSports.com, February 28, 2004.
———. "Advance ticket sales 'mindboggling,'" ChicagoSports.com, March 1, 2004.
Ward, Arch, "In the Wake of the News," *Chicago Tribune*, October 7, 1945.
Weir, Tom, "What the 'hex' is going on," USAToday.com, October 16, 2003.
Wojciechowski, Gene, "Trachsel's goal: Shed goat horns," *Chicago Tribune*, February 19, 1996.
———. "No Joke," ESPN.com, January 21, 2004.
Wolff, Alexander, "Unraveling the Jinx," SportsIllustrated.com, January 15, 2004.
Woodard, Milt, "Trout Puts on His Spectacles Again But the Cubs Really Needed Them," *Chicago Sun*, October 7, 1945.
Yu, Linda, "Has the 'Billy Goat Curse' on the Cubs been lifted?," ABC7Chicago.com, October 3, 2003.

NEWSPAPERS

Chicago Times
Chicago Sun-Times
Chicago Daily Herald
Chicago Tribune
Chicago Herald-American
Daily Illini
San Diego Union-Tribune

INTERNET RESOURCES

ABC7Chicago.com
AndyFrain.com
Baseball-Almanac.com
Baseball-Reference.com
Charleston.com
ChicagoBarProject.com
ChicagoCubs.com
ChicagoSports.com
ChicagoTribune.com
ESPN.com
MLB.com
MercuryNews.com
MiddleTownNews.com
NetShrine.com
SportsIllustrated.com
Sun-Times.com
Times-Union.com
USAToday.com
WGNRadio.com

Index

A

Alfonseca, Antonio 68
Alou, Moises 73
Amalfitano, Joey 36
Ambassador West Hotel 23
Anaheim Angels 65
Andy Frain ushers 3-5
Atlanta Braves 80, 19, 61-62, 64, 70-71, 75-76
Aykroyd, Dan 6

B

Baghdad, Iraq 66
Baker, Dusty 65, 67-68, 70, 74-75
Baltimore Orioles 76
Banks, Ernie 19, 20, 23, 26, 41, 58-59
Bartman, Steve 73
Baseball strike of 1981 36
Baseball strike of 1994 59
Beckert, Glenn 58
Belushi, John 6
Berler, Ron 78
Berardino, Mike 75
Billy Goat Tavern 2, 6, 17, 27, 31, 33, 38, 60-61, 67
Black cat 25, 26-27
Black Sox scandal 77
Bleacher Bums 22-23, 27, 34
Bleacher Bums (play) 54
Boone, Aaron 79
Boston Red Sox 8, 9, 11, 28, 71, 77-79, 80-81
Boudreau, Lou 16
Bragan, Bobby 77
Bridwell, Al 12
Brock, Lou 23
Brooklyn Dodgers 11, 13, 80
Buckner, Bill 38, 78-79

Bush, Joe 9

C

Cabrera, Miguel 74-75
California Angels 28, 33, 42
Camp Ojibwa 24
Caray, Harry 62, 63
Castillo, Luis 73-74
Cey, Ron 37
Chance, Frank 8
Chicago Cubs
    sold 36
Chicago Daily News 34
Chicago Police Sergeants' Association 22
Chicago Sun-Times 20, 58, 59, 70-71, 74
Chicago Times 3
Chicago Tribune 3, 5, 8, 12, 17, 20-21, 23-25, 32-34, 37,
    39-40, 59-60, 62-63, 69, 71, 73-74
Chicago White Sox 21, 32-33, 77, 81
Cincinnati Reds 19, 22, 28, 69
Clark, Will 55
Cleveland Indians 67, 77-78
Colavito, Rocky 78
College of Coaches 16
Colonel Harlan Sanders 78
Colorado Rockies 57
Comiskey Park 8
Condon, David 20-21, 27, 30-31, 34
Craft, Harry 17
Cub power 23-24
Cubs autograph booth 24
Curse of Bobby Bragan 77
Curse of Fred Merkle 11, 13-14, 82
Curse of Rocky Colavito 77
Curse of Shoeless Joe Jackson 77
Curse of the Bambino 9, 71, 77-78, 80-81
Curse of the Billy Goat 5-6, 11, 15-18, 20-21, 25,
    30-35, 40-42, 55, 57-59, 62, 63-65, 67, 70-76
Curse of the Cameramen and Reporters 60
Curse of the Colonel 78

D

Daley, Steve 40
Detroit Tigers 1, 3, 7, 10, 11, 13, 15, 78, 80
Dome hex 21
Dotonbori River 78
Dryden, Charles 12
Durham, Leon 38-39, 79
Durocher, Leo 17, 23-24, 27, 29, 35

E

Eagle River, Wisconsin 24
Eckersley, Dennis 41
Elia, Lee 36
Emslie, Bob 12
Evers, Johnny 8, 12
Ex-Cub Factor 76-77

F

Fabulous Howard's Limousine Service 34
Farnsworth, Kyle 74
Father Guido Sarducci 58
Flag Flu 33
Flood, Curt 22
Florida Marlins 61, 72, 74, 77, 80
Fox, Charlie 36
Frain, Andy 4
Fred Merkle Curse 77
Frey, Jim 37, 40, 53
Frisch, Frankie 16
Fukuoka Daiei Hawks 78

G

Gabor, Zsa Zsa 24
Garvey, Steve 41
Gehrig, Lou 10
Gill, Warren 12
Ginnetti, Toni 58-60
Goatbuster T-shirts 73, 81
Goldblatt, Lynne Walker 23
Gonzalez, Alex 73

Grace, Mark 59
Granger, William 17
Greek Flag Curse 16
Grimm, Charlie 15-16, 30

H

Hall of Fame 19
Hands, Bill 22, 26
Hanshin Tigers 78
Harry Caray Restaurant 62
Hey, Hey! Holy Mackerel 24, 27, 29
Hillis, Elwood Representative 38
Holtzman, Ken 22
Houston Astros 17, 19, 21-22, 28, 66, 68-69, 81
Houston Colt 45's 17

I

Inaugural National League Championship 7
Iraqi War 66
Israel, David 34

J

Jackson, Joe 77
Jenkins, Ferguson 22, 29
John Williams Radio Show 68

K

Kaplan, David 62
Kelly, Ed, Mayor 31
Kentucky Fried Chicken 78
Kessinger, Don 25
Kessler, Gene 3
Knowles, Joe 63

L

Lakeview Baseball Club 65
Lee, Derrek 74
Leno, Jay 6, 57
Lincicome, Bernie 38
Lincoln Tavern 2

Index 113

Lofton, Kenny 67
Logan, Bob 33
Los Angeles Dodgers 19
Lowell, Mike 72

M

MacPhail, Andy 62-63
Magic dust 68
Mariotti, Jay 70-71, 74
Markus, Robert 23-24, 32
Martinez, Pedro 79
Mays, Carl 9
McCarthy, Joe 9
McCormick, Moose 11
McDonough, John 60, 63-64
McGinnity, Joe 12
Merkle, Fred 11-14, 55, 78
Michael, Gene 53
Milwaukee Brewers 42, 68-69
Minute Maid Stadium 68-69
Mitchell, Fred 37
Modified Ex-Cub Factor 78
Montreal Expos 19, 20, 23, 54, 57, 81
Mordecai, Mike 73
Morrissey, Rick 73-74
Munzel, Edward 20
Murphy the goat 2, 3, 32
Murray, Bill 6, 58

N

New York Giants 8, 10-13, 80
New York Mets 17, 19, 23, 25-30, 32, 38, 53-54, 57, 76
New York Times 8, 71
New York Yankees 9, 10, 11, 13, 20, 71, 77, 80
Newman, Loraine 6
Nixon, Richard 20
Novello, Don 58

O

Oakland Athletics 71

O'Day, Hank 12
Olbermann, Keith 13
Old Style Beer 60
Old Style TV commercial 60
"Olympia Restaurant" comic routine 6

P

Patterson, Corey 67
Philadelphia Athletics 8, 10
Philadelphia Phillies 25, 28-29, 34, 54
Pierce, Franklin 8
Pierre, Juan 73
Pittsburgh Pirates 9-13, 19-21, 23, 29-30, 32, 35, 39, 69
Polo Grounds 11
Prell, Edward 25
Prim, Ray 3
Prior, Mark 67, 71, 73-74
Pro Player Stadium 72

R

Ray's Bleachers 34
Reagan, Ronald, President 36
Republican Convention 2
Rituals 79
Rodriguez, Ivan 73-74
Rogers, Phil 69
Royko, Mike 5, 55, 60, 61, 78
Ruth, Babe 8, 9, 10, 80

S

San Diego Padres 19, 41-42, 64, 67, 75
San Francisco Giants 19, 28, 37, 54, 55, 65, 69, 72
Sandberg, Ryne 58
Santo, Ron 25, 60, 69, 72
Saturday Night Live 6
Seaver, Tom 25
Shaughnessy, Dan 80
Sianis, Sam 33-35, 38, 41, 54, 58, 61, 72, 93, 96
Sianis, William "Billy Goat" 2-6, 11, 15-20, 22, 28, 30-31, 33, 60, 70, 81, 87, 88, 90, 93

Smith, Willie 20
Sonovia the goat 31-32
Socrates the goat 34-35, 38
Sonovia the goat 31-32
Sosa, Sammy 59, 62, 66-67, 72
Sports Illustrated 39, 79
Sports Illustrated Cover Curse 39, 77, 79
St. Louis Cardinals 15, 19-20, 22-23, 29, 35, 39, 54, 66-67
State Department 2
Sullivan, Paul 62-63
Superstition in baseball 79
Sutcliffe, Rick 40-41

T

Tampa Bay Devil Rays 66
Texas Rangers 81
Tinker, Joe 8
Tinker to Evers to Chance 8
Tonight Show 6, 57
Torco Oil Sign 38
Toronto Blue Jays 76
Trachsel, Steve 57, 59-60
Trebelhorn, Tom 57-59
Tribune Company 61
        buys Cubs 36
Trout, Paul "Dizzy" 3
Trout, Steve 38
Tyler, Lefty 9

U

Union Station 1, 30

V

Vaughn, Hippo 9
Virgil Homer the goat 68
Vukovich, John 53

W

Walker, Harry 22
Wall of Fame 17
Washington Senators 20

Weeghman Park 8
WGN Television 36
WGN's John Williams Radio Show 68
White Stockings 7
WHO 36
Who Wants to Be a Millionaire? (Television program) 80
Williams, Billy 23
Wilting White Man Theory 67
Wood, Kerry 70-71, 79
Wrigley, Bill 23
Wrigley Building 16
Wrigley Field 2, 4, 8, 10-11, 17, 22, 29, 38, 40, 54, 57, 62, 70, 72, 75, 82
Wrigley Field luxury boxes 54
Wrigley, Philip Knight 16-17, 20, 23-24, 31, 61
Wrigley, William Jr. 8-9, 16, 36

Y

Yankee Stadium 77

Z

Zambrano, Eduardo 59
Zimmer, Don 53

ABOUT THE AUTHOR

Steve Gatto is an attorney who resides in Lansing, Michigan, home of the Chicago Cubs' Class A affiliate the Lansing Lugnuts. He is the author of several non-fiction books including "The Real Wyatt Earp," "Johnny Ringo," and "Curly Bill, Tombstone's Most Famous Outlaw."

Steve was raised in Tucson, Arizona, where he was an avid baseball fan from an early age who would watch Pacific Coast League games during the season and Major League teams in the off-season. Like many Cubs fans, Steve's interest in the Chicago Cubs was passed down from his father, who would watch the Cubbies daily on WGN throughout the 1980s and the 1990s.